Easy 1-2-3® Rele for Windows™

Trudi Reisner
Revised by Janice A. Snyder

Easy 1-2-3 Release 5 for Windows

Library of Congress Catalog No.: 94-67597

ISBN: 1-56529-999-X

97   96   95   94   4   3   2   1

Interpretation of the printing code: the rightmost double-digit number is the year of the book's printing; the rightmost single-digit number, the number of the book's printing. For example, a printing code of 94-1 shows that the first printing of the book occurred in 1994.

Publisher: David P. Ewing

Associate Publisher: Don Roche, Jr.

Managing Editor: Michael Cunningham

Marketing Manager: Greg Wiegand

Associate Product Marketing Manager: Stacy Collins

Credits

Publishing Manager
Nancy Stevenson

Acquisitions Editor
Thomas F. Godfrey III

Product Director
Joyce J. Nielsen

Production Editor
Thomas F. Hayes

Copy Editors
Lisa Gebken
Nicole Rodandello

Technical Editor
Warren W. Estep

Book Designer
Amy Peppler-Adams

Cover Designer
Jay Corpus

Production Team
Steve Adams
Stephen Carlin
Amy Cornwell
Karen Dodson
Chad Dressler
Bob LaRoche
Beth Lewis
Steph Mineart
Nanci Sears Perry
Mike Thomas
Tina Trettin

Indexer
Michael Hughes

Composed in *Stone Serif* and *MCPdigital* by Que Corporation

About the Authors

Trudi Reisner is a computer consultant specializing in training users of IBM PCs, PC compatibles, and Apple Macintoshes in the use of applications software. She is the owner of Computer Training Solutions, a Boston, Mass., company that offers training, technical writing, curriculum development, and consulting services in software programs. Trudi has written many books on Windows and other software including Que's *Ami Pro 3 Quick Reference*; *Easy 1-2-3 Release 4 for Windows*; *Easy Excel 5 for Windows*; *Easy Word 6 for Windows*, Second Edition; *Easy WordPerfect 6 for Windows*, Second Edition; *Excel VisiRef*; and *Word for Windows 2 Quick Reference*.

Janice A. Snyder is an independent consultant specializing in microcomputer software applications. She has worked with 1-2-3 spreadsheets for 10 years, since the days of Release 1A. As director of the Administrative Computer Center at Indiana Wesleyan University for three years, she managed PC support and directed the successful implementation of a new administrative software system. She co-authored Que's *Excel 5 for Windows Quick Reference,* Special Edition, revised *1-2-3 Release 5 for Windows Quick Reference,* and edited *I Hate 1-2-3 (Release 4) for Windows*. Snyder lives in Virginia Beach, VA, having recently moved from "Que territory" in Indiana.

Trademark Acknowledgments

Contents at a Glance

Contents

Part III: Working with Formulas   82

Part IV: Managing Files   114

Part V: Formatting the Worksheet   134

Part VI: Printing the Worksheet 168

Part VII: Working with Charts and Maps 186

Part VIII: Sample Documents 220

Part IX: Reference 232

Index 238

Introduction

Introduction

Lotus 1-2-3 for Windows is one of the world's most popular spreadsheet software programs. Although you could create worksheets on ledger paper and use a calculator, or draw charts on graph paper, 1-2-3 makes managing numeric information much easier. You can use the program to create worksheets, databases, charts, and macros.

Specifically, you can use 1-2-3 to perform these functions:

- **Lay out a worksheet.** When you sit down to develop a worksheet with a pencil and ledger paper, you don't always have all the information to complete the design and layout of the worksheet. Ideas may occur to you after you sketch the layout. After you're finished jotting down the column headings and the row headings, you may think of another column or row you didn't include. With 1-2-3, you can insert columns and rows easily and move data from one location to another. You can begin with a blank worksheet, or get an instant worksheet layout using the new SmartMasters templates.

- **Calculate numbers.** If you have a checkbook register, you subtract the amount of each check written and add the deposits to the running balance. When you receive your bank statement and balance your checkbook, you may find that you made math errors in your checkbook. In this case, you must erase the old answers, recalculate the numbers, and jot down the new answers. In 1-2-3, you enter a formula once. Then, when you change the numbers in the worksheet, 1-2-3 recalculates the formulas instantly and gives you the new answers.

- **Make editing changes.** To correct a mistake on ledger paper, you have to use an eraser or reconstruct the entire worksheet. With 1-2-3, you can overwrite data in any cell in your worksheet. You also can delete data quickly in one cell or a range of cells.

- **Undo mistakes.** When you accidentally delete data you want to keep, you don't have to retype it. Instead, you can restore the data with the Undo feature. You also can use the Undo command to reverse the last command or action.

- **Check spelling.** Before you print, you can run a spell check to search for misspellings. If you are a poor typist, this feature enables you to concentrate on calculating your numbers and lets 1-2-3 catch your spelling errors.

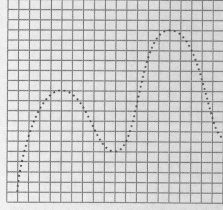

- **View data.** When working with a large worksheet, such as a financial statement, you may have to use a ruler to compare figures on a remote portion of the worksheet on ledger paper. In 1-2-3, you can split the worksheet into two panes to view distant figures side-by-side. That way, you can easily see the effects of playing "what if?" scenarios to project changes and then make the necessary adjustments.

- **Make formatting changes.** 1-2-3 easily enables you to align data in cells; center column headings across columns; adjust column widths; display numbers with dollar signs, commas, and decimal points; and use other formatting options. You can experiment with the settings until the worksheet appears the way that you want it. Then you can print it.

- **Change how data is printed.** You can boldface, italicize, and underline data. 1-2-3 also lets you shade or color cells and add borders. You can also use a different typeface and change the color of text, depending on your printer's capabilities.

- **Preview your print job.** You can preview your worksheet to see how it will look when it is printed. If you want to make changes to the page setup before you print, you also can do this by using the Page Setup SmartIcon in Print Preview.

- **Sort data.** You can sort data on the worksheet alphabetically and numerically in ascending or descending order. You can, for example, sort a customer invoice report in chronological order by dates.

- **Chart numeric data.** You can track the sales trends of several products with an embedded bar chart. Make as many "what if?" projections as you want in the worksheet by increasing and decreasing the numbers. As you change the numbers in the worksheet, 1-2-3 instantly updates the embedded chart.1-2-3's embedded charts let you view simultaneously the sales trends in a picture representation on-screen and the numbers in the worksheet, making your sales forecasting more efficient. You also can link worksheet data to a geographic map.

- **Share data.** If you are using 1-2-3 for Windows on a network with Lotus Notes or electronic mail installed, you can exchange worksheet data with other users on the network.

Introduction

Task Sections

The Task sections include numbered steps that tell you how to accomplish certain tasks, such as saving a worksheet or filling a range. The numbered steps walk you through a specific example so that you learn by doing.

Big Screen

At the beginning of each task is a large screen shot that shows how the computer screen will look after you complete the procedure in that task. Sometimes, however, the screen shot shows a feature discussed in that task, such as a shortcut menu.

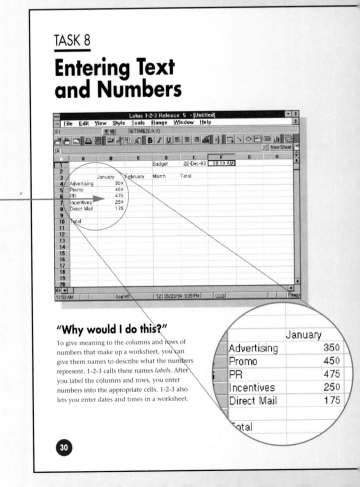

TASK 8

Entering Text and Numbers

"Why would I do this?"

To give meaning to the columns and rows of numbers that make up a worksheet, you can give them names to describe what the numbers represent. 1-2-3 calls these names *labels*. After you label the columns and rows, you enter numbers into the appropriate cells. 1-2-3 also lets you enter dates and times in a worksheet.

30

Step-by-Step Screens

Each task includes a screen shot for each step. The screen shot shows how the computer screen looks at each step in the process. Some screens include one or more red circles that indicate parts of the screen affected by the corresponding step.

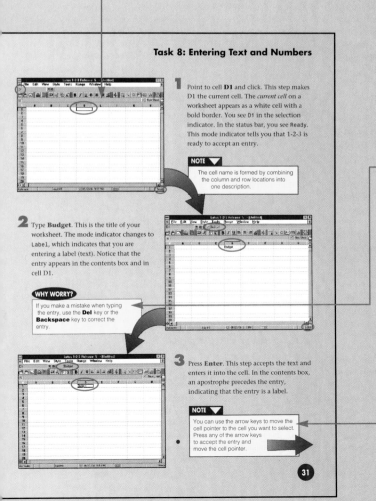

Task 8: Entering Text and Numbers

1 Point to cell **D1** and click. This step makes D1 the current cell. The *current cell* on a worksheet appears as a white cell with a bold border. You see D1 in the selection indicator. In the status bar, you see Ready. This mode indicator tells you that 1-2-3 is ready to accept an entry.

NOTE ▼
The cell name is formed by combining the column and row locations into one description.

2 Type **Budget**. This is the title of your worksheet. The mode indicator changes to Label, which indicates that you are entering a label (text). Notice that the entry appears in the contents box and in cell D1.

WHY WORRY?
If you make a mistake when typing the entry, use the **Del** key or the **Backspace** key to correct the entry.

3 Press **Enter**. This step accepts the text and enters it into the cell. In the contents box, an apostrophe precedes the entry, indicating that the entry is a label.

NOTE ▼
You can use the arrow keys to move the cell pointer to the cell you want to select. Press any of the arrow keys to accept the entry and move the cell pointer.

31

Why Worry? Notes

You may find that you performed a task, such as sorting data, that you didn't want to do after all. The Why Worry? notes tell you how to undo certain procedures or how to get out of a situation, such as displaying a Help screen.

Other Notes

Many tasks include other short notes that tell you a little more about certain procedures. These notes define terms, explain other options, refer you to other sections when applicable, and so on.

PART I
The Basics

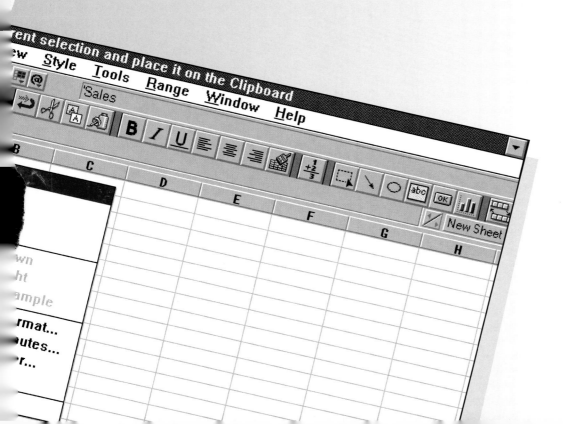

Part I: The Basics

Part I of this book introduces you to 1-2-3 basics. You need to know some fundamental things about 1-2-3 before you start creating your own worksheets.

In this part, you learn how to start and exit 1-2-3. You should have 1-2-3 installed on your hard disk so that it appears in your Windows Program Manager as a program icon. For instructions, refer to your Lotus 1-2-3 Release 5 for Windows documentation.

A *worksheet* is a grid of columns and rows. The intersection of any column and row is called a *cell*. Each cell in a worksheet has a unique cell address. A cell address is the designation formed by combining the row and column names. For example, A8 is the address of the cell at the intersection of column A and row 8.

A *range* is a specified group of cells. A range can be a single cell, a column, a row, or any combination of cells, columns, and rows. *Range coordinates* identify a range. The first element in the range coordinates is the location of the uppermost left cell in the range; the second element is the location of the lowermost right cell. Two periods separate these two elements. For example, the range A1..C3 includes the cells A1, A2, A3, B1, B2, B3, C1, C2, and C3.

You use the *cell pointer* to select any cell in the worksheet. The selected cell is called the *current cell*. The current cell contains the cell pointer—a dark border around the cell. You always have at least one cell selected at all times. In this part, you are shown how to select a single cell, a group of cells (called a *range*), and multiple ranges.

You can navigate around the worksheet with the following direction keys and key combinations:

To Move	Press
Right one cell	→
Left one cell	←
Right one screen	**Tab**
Left one screen	**Shift**+**Tab**
Up one row	↑
Down one row	↓

To Move	Press
To the beginning of a row	**End+←**
To the end of a row	**End+→**
To the first cell (A1)	**Ctrl+Home**
To the last cell (containing data)	**End Home**

You can make different sheets visible by scrolling through sheets within a worksheet file. You can work only on the top sheet. This sheet is called the *active sheet*. To determine which sheet is active, just look at the worksheet tabs that appear below the SmartIcons and above the worksheet's column border. The current worksheet's tab is emphasized with a 3-D border. You can change the name or color of any worksheet tab. The worksheet's letter also appears in the top left corner of the worksheet, just below the worksheet tab.

You also learn how to use the quick menus. Quick menus contain fewer commands than a menu in the menu bar. The commands on the quick menus vary, depending on the cells or object you select in the worksheet.

SmartIcons enable you to instantly select a command or perform a task. 1-2-3 ships with eight sets of SmartIcons that contain the tools you use for creating a chart, drawing graphics on the worksheet, creating macros, and many other 1-2-3 operations.

There are a multitude of ways to get help in 1-2-3. You can:

- Get instant on-line help

- Display Help topic categories in Help's table of contents

- Search for Help topics in the Search dialog box

- Look at the keyboard shortcuts

- View the How Do I? list of common 1-2-3 tasks

You also can choose For Upgraders in the Help menu to find out about 1-2-3's new features, 1-2-3 Classic, and parts of the 1-2-3 window.

The tasks that follow in this part teach essential skills you need to perform many of 1-2-3's operations.

Starting and Exiting 1-2-3 for Windows

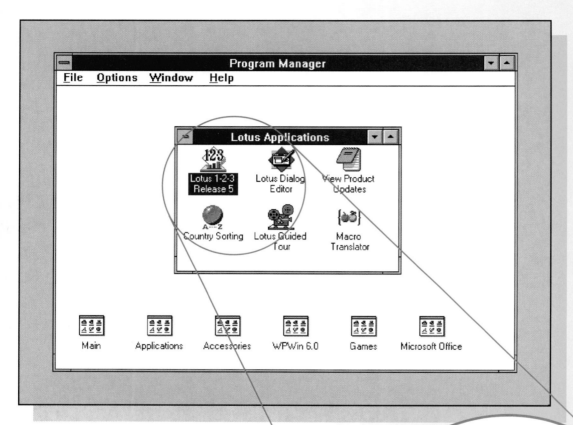

"Why would I do this?"

Starting 1-2-3 is simple to do—once you have done it, it is as easy as starting the engine in your car. When you no longer want to work in 1-2-3, you can exit 1-2-3 and return to the Windows Program Manager. This task assumes that you have turned on your computer and monitor and started Microsoft Windows. The Program Manager appears in a window on-screen.

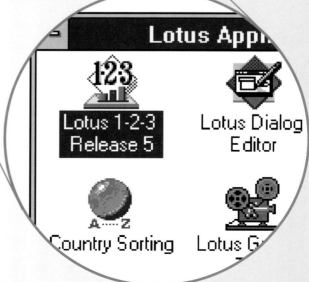

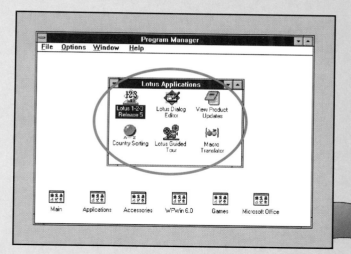

1 Double-click the group icon for Lotus Applications. To double-click the group icon, move the mouse pointer to the group icon and click the left mouse button twice in rapid succession. This opens the Lotus Applications window.

NOTE ▼

If the program is maximized, you only need to click the existing program group to make it active.

2 Double-click the program icon for Lotus 1-2-3 Release 5. This step starts the 1-2-3 program. The Welcome to 1-2-3 dialog box appears in front of a blank worksheet.

NOTE ▼

Before you exit 1-2-3, save any worksheets you have changed. If you typed any data or made changes to the worksheet, 1-2-3 prompts you to save the changes.

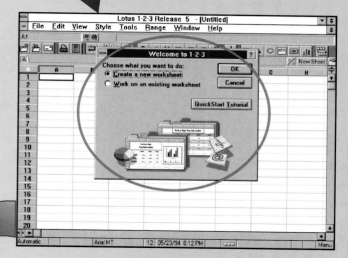

3 Click **File** in the menu bar. Then, click **Exit**. This step selects the File Exit command. You return to the Windows Program Manager.

NOTE ▼

To quickly exit 1-2-3, double-click the **Control** menu box. This box appears to the left of the 1-2-3 window's title bar, in the upper left corner of the screen.

Using Quick Menus and SmartIcons

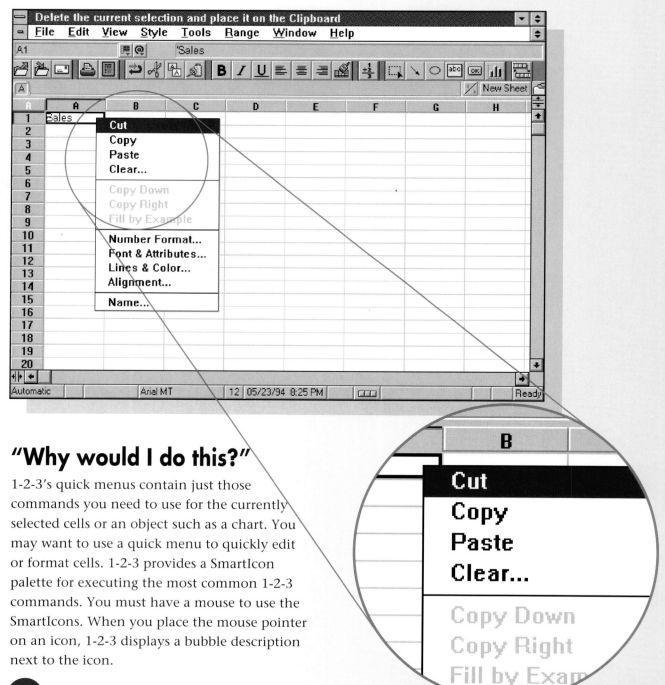

"Why would I do this?"

1-2-3's quick menus contain just those commands you need to use for the currently selected cells or an object such as a chart. You may want to use a quick menu to quickly edit or format cells. 1-2-3 provides a SmartIcon palette for executing the most common 1-2-3 commands. You must have a mouse to use the SmartIcons. When you place the mouse pointer on an icon, 1-2-3 displays a bubble description next to the icon.

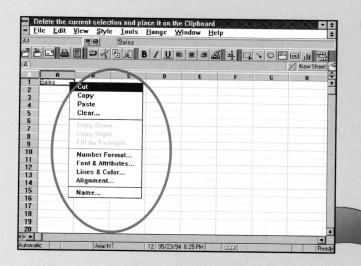

1 Point to the inside of cell **A1** and click the right mouse button. This action opens the quick menu. 1-2-3 displays a list of editing and formatting commands.

2 Click **Clear** to select the Clear command. The quick menu disappears. 1-2-3 opens the Clear dialog box.

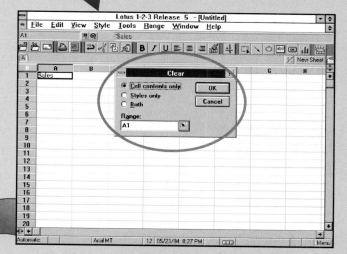

3 Click **OK**. This step clears the cell contents.

WHY WORRY?

Sometimes you may display a quick menu that doesn't have the command you want to use. To leave a quick menu without making a selection, press **Esc**.

Task 2: Using Quick Menus and SmartIcons

4 Point to the **Open File** SmartIcon, the first icon on the left side of the SmartIcon palette. The icon's description appears in a bubble next to the icon.

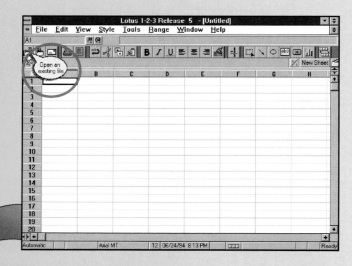

5 Click the **Open File** SmartIcon. The Open File dialog box appears.

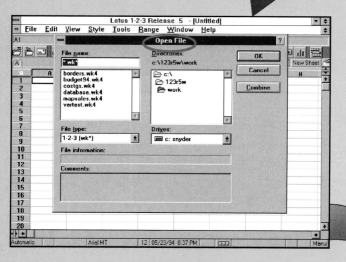

6 Click the **Cancel** button in the dialog box. 1-2-3 closes the Open File dialog box.

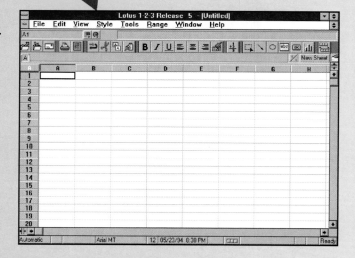

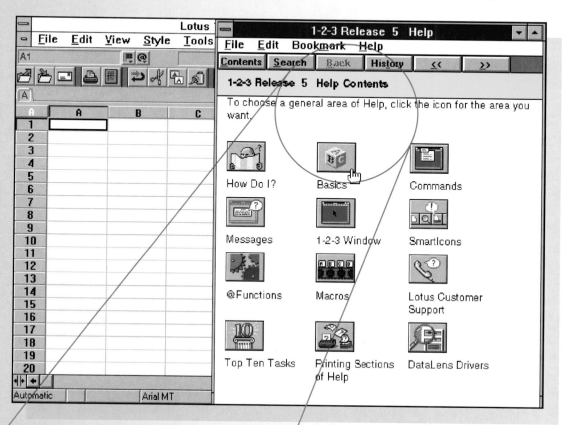

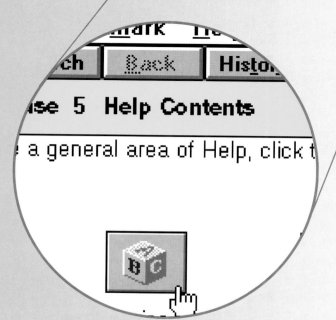

"Why would I do this?"

1-2-3 offers many ways to get help, and the Help feature has its own menu system. The Help feature is particularly useful when you don't remember how to complete a task in 1-2-3 or when you want to learn more about 1-2-3.

Task 3: Getting Help

1 Click **Help** in the menu bar, and then click **Contents**; or press **F1**. 1-2-3 opens the Help window. The name of the Help window appears in the title bar. You see the icons for Help topics.

NOTE ▼

When the mouse pointer is placed on a Help icon, the pointer changes to a hand with a pointing finger.

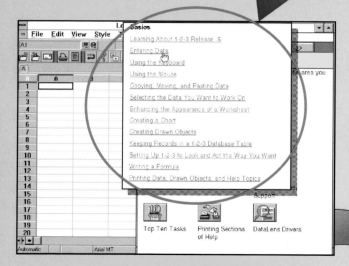

2 Point to **Basics** and click the left mouse button. This selects the category for which you want help. A list of topics appears.

3 Point to the topic **Entering Data** and click the left mouse button. Information about entering data appears on-screen.

NOTE ▼

You may have to scroll the Help window to see all the information.

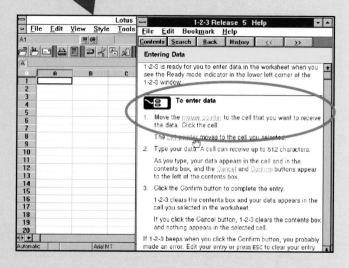

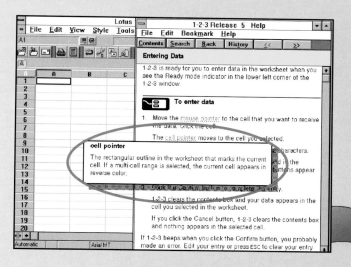

4 Point to the green underlined term **cell pointer** and click the left mouse button. This step displays the definition in a box. Click anywhere to close it.

5 Click **File** in the Help window's menu bar.

> **NOTE** ▼
>
> You also can double-click the **Control** menu box in the upper left corner of the Help window to close the Help window.

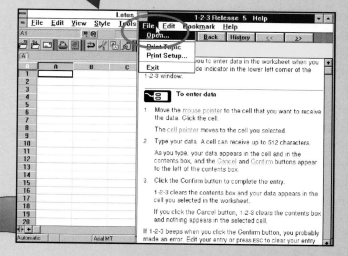

6 Click **Exit**. This selects the File Exit command and closes the Help window.

> **NOTE** ▼
>
> You also can click the **Help** button in a dialog box (the button with a question mark in the upper right corner of a dialog box) to get help on the command for which you are setting options.

TASK 4

Moving around the Worksheet

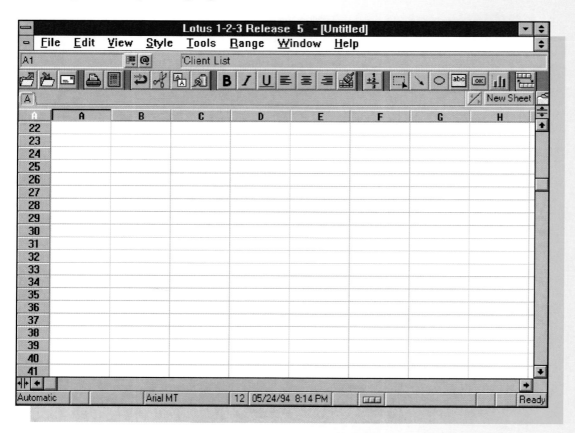

"Why would I do this?"

With so many cells, you need a shortcut for moving around the worksheet. Using a mouse is often the easiest way to move around the worksheet—simply use the vertical or horizontal scroll bar to move to other portions of the worksheet.

18

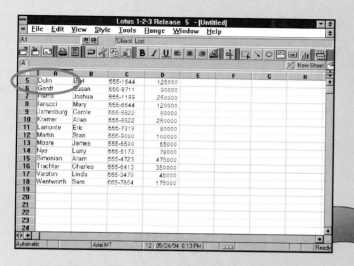

1 Click the down scroll arrow at the bottom of the vertical scroll bar four times. Row 5 appears at the top of the worksheet. Click the up scroll arrow at the top of the vertical scroll bar three times. Row 2 appears at the top of the worksheet.

NOTE ▼
You can point to the up, down, left, or right scroll bar arrow and hold down the mouse button to scroll the worksheet continuously in a particular direction.

2 Click halfway down in the vertical scroll bar. This step moves the worksheet up or down one screen at a time. Notice that row 22 appears at the top of the worksheet. Your screen may look different, depending on where you clicked.

NOTE ▼
You also can press the **PgDn** key or the **PgUp** key to move down or up one screen at a time.

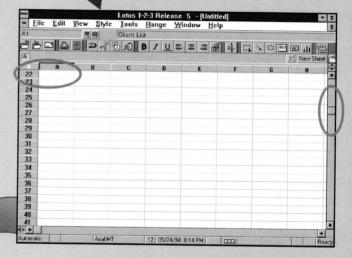

3 Drag the scroll box up to the top of the vertical scroll bar. Dragging the scroll box moves the worksheet quickly to a new location in the direction of the scroll box.

NOTE ▼
Keep in mind that whatever scroll bar action you perform on a vertical scroll bar can be performed the same way on the horizontal scroll bar.

Moving between Worksheets

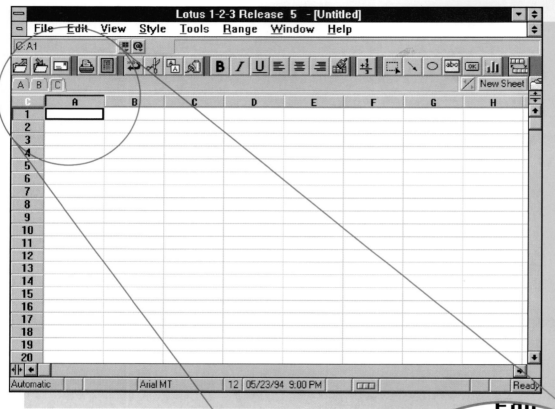

"Why would I do this?"

Suppose that all the sheets relating to inventory are stored in one worksheet file. Before you can make changes to these sheets, you need to move from sheet to sheet to find the one you want to view or change. You can use the scroll tabs to move between worksheets. After you make a sheet visible, you can select it so that you can work on the sheet.

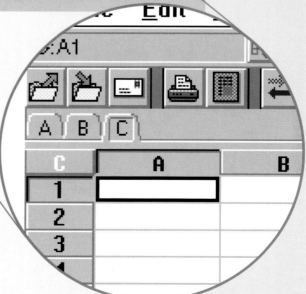

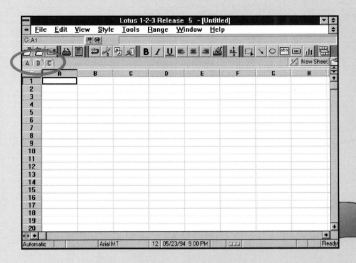

1 Click the **New Sheet** button twice. Clicking the New Sheet button inserts a new sheet on top of any existing sheets. In this case, clicking twice inserts sheets B and C. Worksheet tab C is currently highlighted, making it the active sheet.

2 Click worksheet tab **A**. 1-2-3 moves this sheet to the top and makes it the active sheet.

NOTE ▼

You can use the tab scroll arrows if you have so many worksheets that you cannot see their tabs on-screen at once. The tab scroll arrows appear just left of the New Sheet button.

WHY WORRY?

If you selected the wrong sheet, just click the correct worksheet tab.

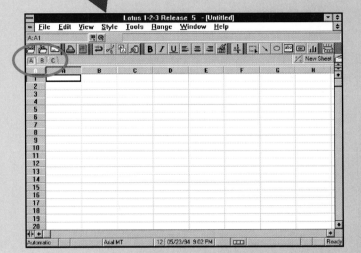

Moving to a Specific Cell

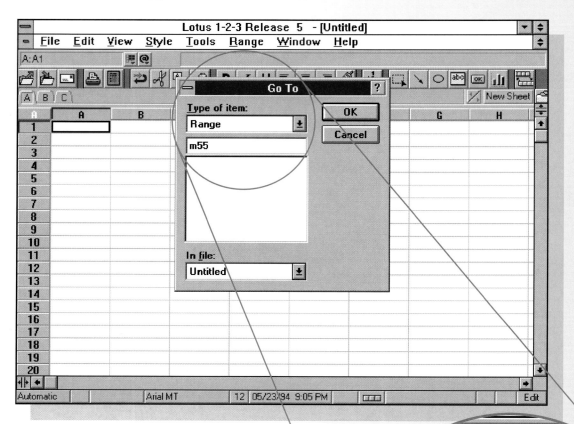

"Why would I do this?"

The Go To command is useful for jumping to cells that are out of view. You can also use the Go To command to select a range of cells. A range of cells is referenced by its first and last cells, separated by two periods. For example, B5..E8 references the upper left cell B5 and the lower right cell E8.

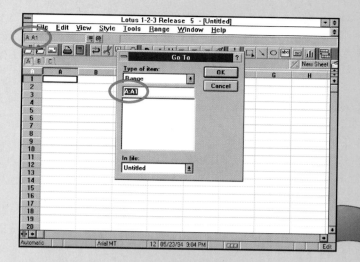

1 Press **F5**. F5 is the Go To key. Pressing F5 selects the Go To command. 1-2-3 opens the Go To dialog box. A:A1 appears in the text box. This cell is the current cell.

2 Type **M55**. M55 is the cell to which you want to go. Remember that cells are referenced by their column letter and row number.

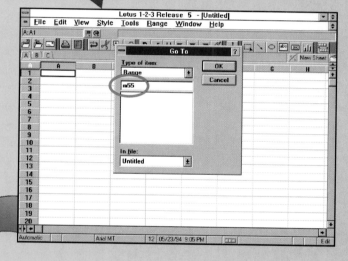

3 Press **Enter**. When you press Enter, M55 becomes the current cell.

WHY WORRY?

If you mistakenly moved to the wrong cell reference, repeat the Go To command to move to the correct cell. If you selected the wrong range, click any cell to deselect the range. Then try again.

Selecting Cells

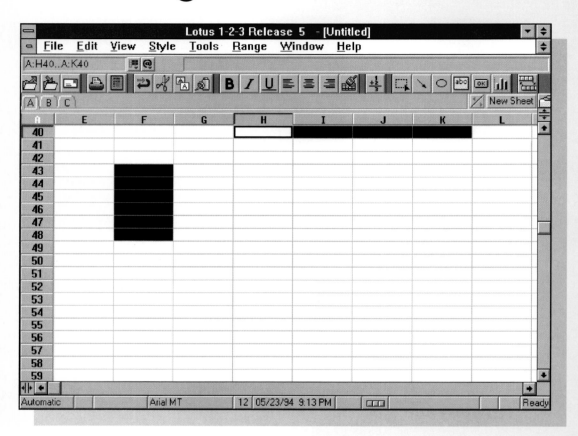

"Why would I do this?"

Most of the commands and options in 1-2-3
operate on a selected cell. You can also select
a *range*, or a group of adjacent cells. You can
even select several ranges at one time with the
mouse. For example, you may want to perform
a command on a group of cells that are not
adjacent. Suppose that you want to change
the alignment of text in the top row of the
worksheet and a column along the side. To
make the change to both ranges, you need
to select both ranges at the same time.

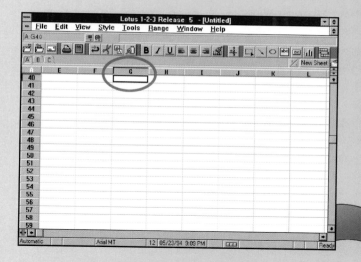

1 Click cell **G40**. G40 becomes the current cell.

2 Hold down the mouse button and drag the mouse to select cells **F43**, **F44**, **F45**, **F46**, **F47**, and **F48**. This deselects cell G40 and selects the range F43..F48.

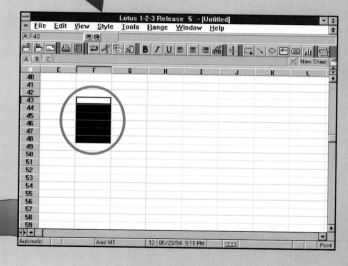

3 Hold down the Ctrl key and drag the mouse to select cells **H40**, **I40**, **J40**, and **K40**. Release the mouse button, and then release the Ctrl key. Notice that both ranges remain selected.

WHY WORRY?

If you selected the wrong cell, simply click the correct cell. If you selected the wrong range of cells, just click any cell to deselect the range. Then start over.

PART II

Entering and Editing Data

Part II: Entering and Editing Data

There are four types of data you can enter into a 1-2-3 worksheet: text, numbers, calculations, and dates. Text entries are called *labels*. 1-2-3 aligns labels with the left side of a cell. Labels contain alphabetic characters, other symbols, or both letters and numbers. When a text entry contains numbers, 1-2-3 cannot use it for numeric calculations.

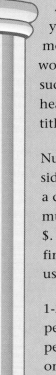

An example of a label is a title that describes the type of worksheet you want to create. A title such as 1994 ANNUAL BUDGET gives meaning to the columns and rows of numbers that make up a budget worksheet. You can enter column headings to specify time periods such as years, months, days, dates, and so on. You can enter row headings to identify income and expense items in a budget, subject titles, and other categories.

Numeric entries are called *values*. 1-2-3 aligns values with the right side of a cell. Values contain numbers and other symbols. Numeric entries must begin with a numeral or one of the following symbols: + − . (or $. The period is used as a decimal point for decimal values. You may find it quicker to enter numeric data by typing the numbers and using the Enter key on your numeric keypad.

1-2-3's Undo command lets you reverse almost any operation you perform. You must select the Undo command immediately after performing the action you want to undo—before doing further work on the worksheet. Undo undoes the preceding operation.

You can easily erase the contents of a cell by using the Del key. 1-2-3 also lets you erase a range of cells.

1-2-3's Copy command lets you copy one cell to another cell. 1-2-3 lets you copy labels, values, and formulas. When you copy data in a cell, the original data remains intact and a duplicate is placed in a new location. You also can copy one cell to a group of cells and copy more than one cell (a range).

When you insert cells, rows, or columns in your worksheet, you will not lose your existing data. For example, when you insert a row, all rows below it shift down to make room. When you insert a row, 1-2-3 does not automatically copy any cell formats to the new row. You must format all the columns in the row.

When you delete cells, rows, or columns in your worksheet, 1-2-3 shifts the existing cells, rows, or columns to close up the space. When you delete a row or a column, you delete all the data in that row or column—including any data that is off-screen. Be sure to examine the entire row or column before you delete it.

The View Zoom In command lets you enlarge the display of your worksheet by 10% each time you select the command. This command magnifies the view of your worksheet as much as 400%. The View Zoom Out command lets you shrink the display of your worksheet by 10% each time you select the command. Zooming out reduces the view of your worksheet to as little as 25% of the normal size. The normal size (default magnification percentage setting) is 87%.

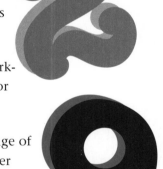

When you scroll a large worksheet, you may find that the column and row titles shift off-screen. To keep the titles on-screen as you scroll, you can use the View Freeze Titles command. This feature freezes column and row titles so that when you scroll to other areas of the worksheet, the titles remain on-screen.

The Find & Replace feature lets you replace data that affects the whole worksheet. You can specify many search options, look through all worksheets or only the selected range, or find data in labels, formulas, or both.

1-2-3's spell checker lets you check for spelling errors in a single cell, a range of cells, an entire worksheet, or a chart. You can add your own words to a user dictionary, check for capitalization errors and duplicate occurrences of a word (such as *the the*), and search for words with numbers (such as *1st, 2nd*).

The 1-2-3 data-entry techniques and editing commands that you will learn in this part will save you time and effort when creating your worksheets.

Entering Text and Numbers

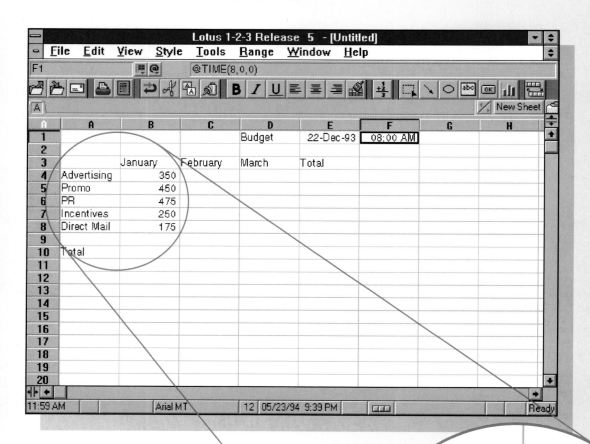

"Why would I do this?"

To give meaning to the columns and rows of numbers that make up a worksheet, you can give them names to describe what the numbers represent. 1-2-3 calls these names *labels*. After you label the columns and rows, you enter numbers into the appropriate cells. 1-2-3 also lets you enter dates and times in a worksheet.

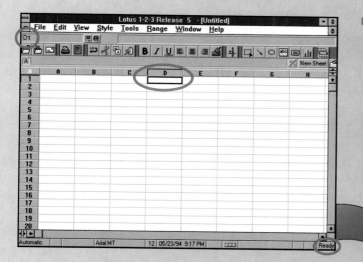

1 Point to cell **D1** and click. This step makes D1 the current cell. The *current cell* on a worksheet appears as a white cell with a bold border. You see D1 in the selection indicator. In the status bar, you see Ready. This mode indicator tells you that 1-2-3 is ready to accept an entry.

NOTE ▼

The cell name is formed by combining the column and row locations into one description.

2 Type **Budget**. This is the title of your worksheet. The mode indicator changes to Label, which indicates that you are entering a label (text). Notice that the entry appears in the contents box and in cell D1.

WHY WORRY?

If you make a mistake when typing the entry, use the **Del** key or the **Backspace** key to correct the entry.

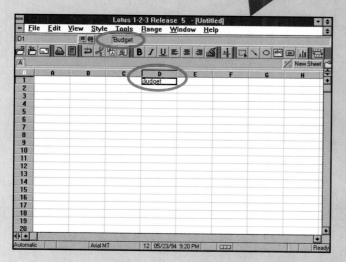

3 Press **Enter**. This step accepts the text and enters it into the cell. In the contents box, an apostrophe precedes the entry, indicating that the entry is a label.

NOTE ▼

You can use the arrow keys to move the cell pointer to the cell you want to select. Press any of the arrow keys to accept the entry and move the cell pointer.

31

Task 8: Entering Text and Numbers

4 Select cell **B3**. This cell is where you will enter a label for the first column heading.

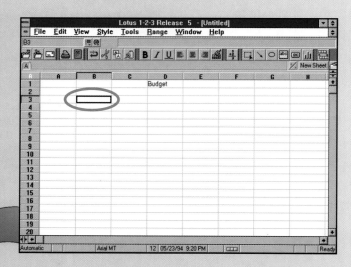

5 Type **January** and press the right-arrow key (→). Pressing the right-arrow key accepts the entry, enters the label into the cell, and moves the cell pointer to cell C3. Notice that January is left-aligned. This alignment is the default format for labels.

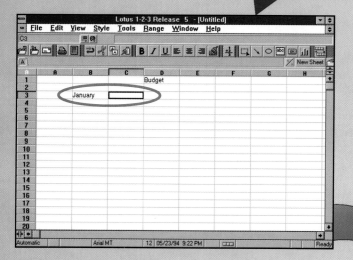

6 Type **February** and press the right-arrow key (→). Pressing the right-arrow key accepts the entry, enters the label into the cell, and moves the cell pointer to cell D3.

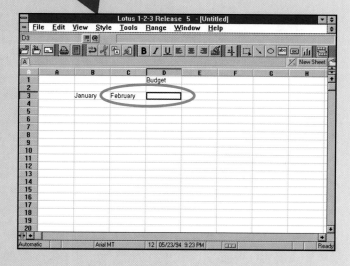

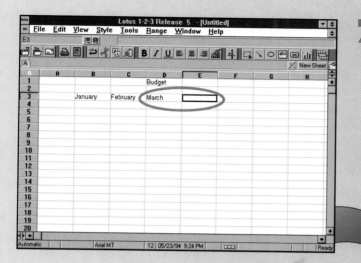

7 Type **March** and press the right-arrow key (→). Pressing the right-arrow key accepts the entry, enters the label into the cell, and moves the cell pointer to cell E3.

8 Type **Total** and press **Enter**. Pressing Enter accepts the entry in the contents box and enters it into the cell. The cell pointer remains in cell E3.

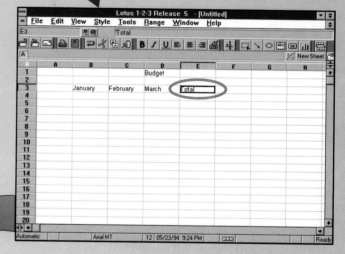

9 Starting in cell **A4**, type the remaining data that appears in the figure. When you type a number into a cell, the mode indicator changes to Value.

10 Click cell **E1**, type **@DATE(93,12,22)**, and then press **Enter**. The number 34325 appears, which is a serial representation of the date.

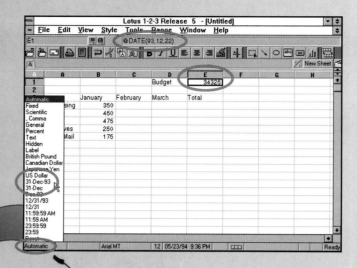

11 Click the list in the status bar. The number format list is the first panel in the status bar and displays Automatic. You see a list of number formats. Click the format **31-Dec-93**. In the cell, you see 22-Dec-93.

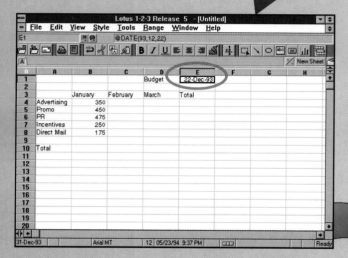

> **NOTE** ▼
>
> If asterisks (*) appear in the column, the entry is too large. Change the column width.

12 Click cell **F1**, type **@TIME(8,0,0)**, and then press **Enter**. Next, click the **number format** list in the status bar. The number format list is the first panel in the status bar and displays Automatic. You see a list of number formats. Click the format: **11:59 AM**. In the cell, you see 08:00 AM.

> **WHY WORRY?**
>
> To delete the most recent entry, click the **Undo** SmartIcon.

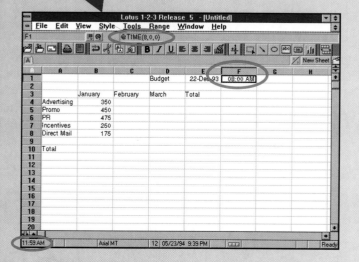

Using Undo

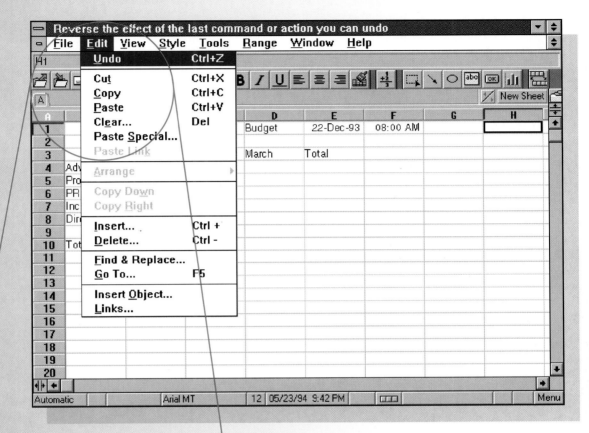

"Why would I do this?"

The Undo feature recovers the most recent changes to worksheet data. For instance, if you edit the worksheet and make a mistake, you can use Undo to reverse the last editing command you performed. Undo becomes very helpful when you need to correct editing and formatting mistakes, especially when you delete data you did not intend to delete. 1-2-3 can restore deleted data with Undo.

Task 9: Using Undo

1 Click cell **F1**. Then, press **Del**. This step removes the time entry in cell F1. This is the entry you want to restore with Undo.

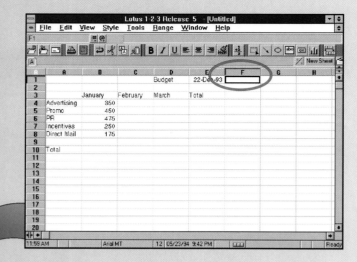

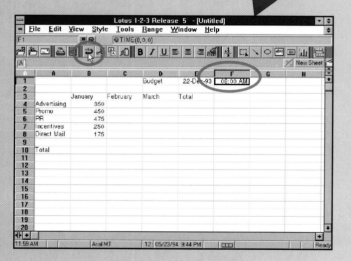

2 Click the **Undo** SmartIcon. This step selects the Edit Undo command. 1-2-3 restores the entry in cell F1. As you can see, the worksheet returns to its preceding form.

WHY WORRY?

If you click the **Edit** menu and notice that the Undo command is gray, you cannot undo the task. Not all tasks can be undone.

Overwriting a Cell

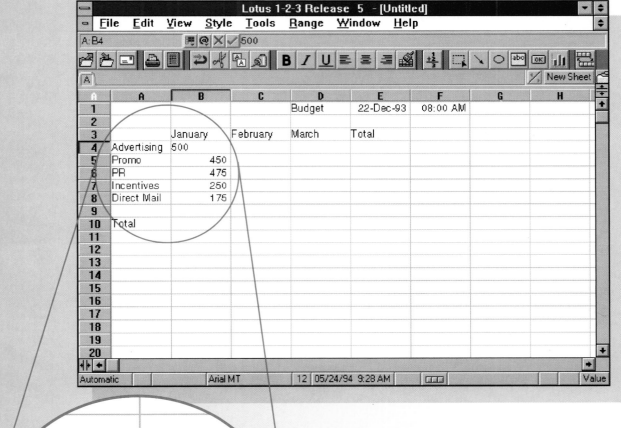

"Why would I do this?"

Overwriting a cell means replacing the existing contents of a cell with new data. If the change is minor, you can edit the cell's contents instead. Overwriting a cell is handy when you want to correct typing errors or when a cell contains the wrong data. You also may want to play "what if" scenarios. For example, what if you want to forecast the profit if you increase the income? What if you run more ads for two months or you intensify your direct mail campaign?

Task 10: Overwriting a Cell

1 Click cell **B4** to make it the current cell. The contents box displays the current entry—the entry you want to overwrite. The mode indicator displays Ready.

WHY WORRY?

If you make a mistake, use **Del** or **Backspace** to correct the entry.

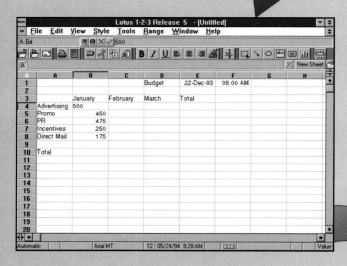

2 Type **500**. The new entry, 500, appears in the contents box and in the cell.

NOTE ▼

Be careful not to overwrite formulas with labels or values if that is not what you intend. If you overwrite a formula with a value, 1-2-3 no longer updates the formula.

3 Press **Enter** to replace the previous entry with the new entry. Before you press Enter, you can press the **Esc** key to cancel the changes.

WHY WORRY?

To restore the original cell contents, click the **Undo** SmartIcon immediately after you overwrite the cell.

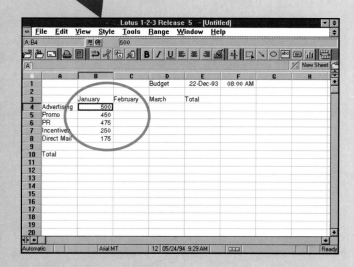

Editing a Cell

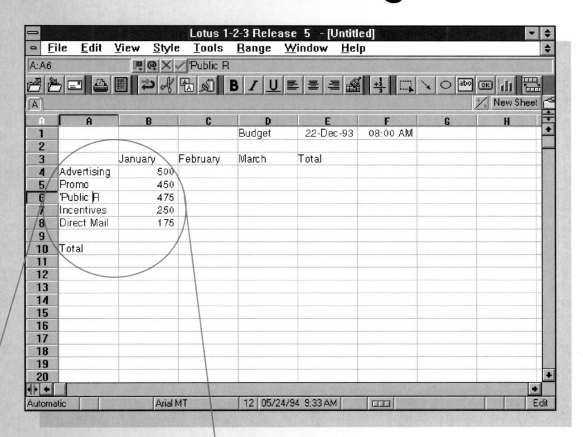

"Why would I do this?"

By editing a cell, you can correct data after it is placed in a cell. You can make changes to part or all of the information in a cell. After you know how to edit your data, you won't have to type an entire entry over again. You can just make a few quick changes to correct the contents of a cell. If the new entry is entirely different, overwrite the entry instead.

Task 11: Editing a Cell

1 Double-click cell **A6**. Double-clicking a cell allows you to edit the data right in the cell. 1-2-3 moves the insertion point to the end of the entry in the cell—the entry you want to change.

> **NOTE** ▼
>
> You also can click the contents box. This moves the cursor to the contents box. An X and a check mark appear before the entry. (Clicking the X cancels the change; clicking the check mark confirms the new entry.)

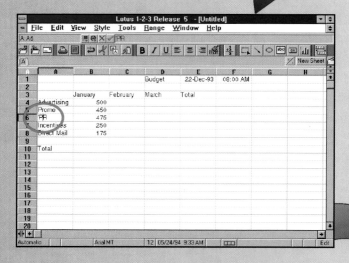

2 Press the left-arrow key (←). This moves the insertion point to the letter R. You can use the arrow keys to move the cursor to the characters you want to change or delete. You can use the **Home** key to move the insertion point to the beginning of the entry.

3 Type **ublic**, and then press the space bar. Typing in Edit mode inserts characters. This entry changes the row label from PR to Public R.

> **NOTE** ▼
>
> You can use the **Ins** key to overwrite characters in Edit mode. You also can use the **Del** or **Backspace** key to delete characters.

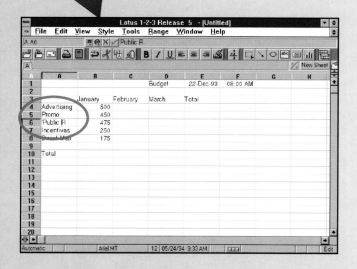

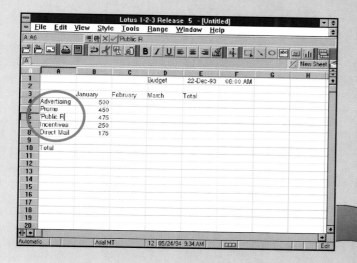

4 Press **End**. Pressing End in Edit mode moves the insertion point to the end of the entry.

5 Type **elations**. This entry changes the label to Public Relations.

NOTE ▼

Before you press **Enter** to accept the entry, you can press the **Esc** key to cancel the changes.

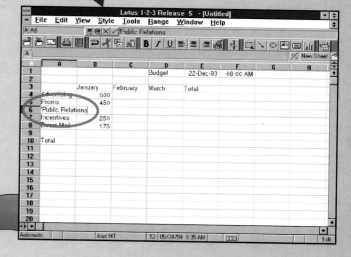

6 Press **Enter**. This accepts the new entry. Notice that only part of the long entry appears in cell A6. The column is not wide enough to accommodate this long entry. You can widen the column so that the entire label appears in the column.

Task 11: Editing a Cell

7 Double-click cell **A5**. This moves the insertion point to the end of the entry in the cell—the entry you want to change.

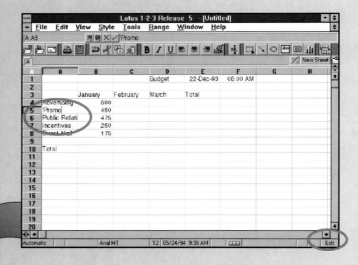

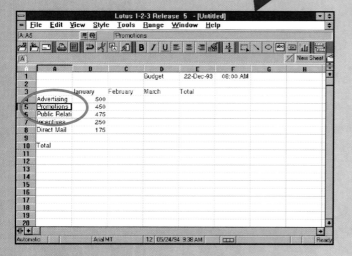

8 Type **tions**, and then press **Enter**. This changes the row label Promo to Promotions. Before you press Enter, you can press the **Esc** key to cancel the changes.

WHY WORRY?

To undo the edit, click the **Undo** SmartIcon immediately after editing the cell.

Erasing a Cell

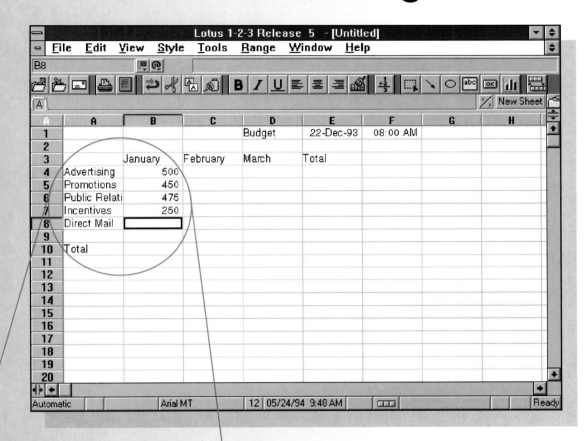

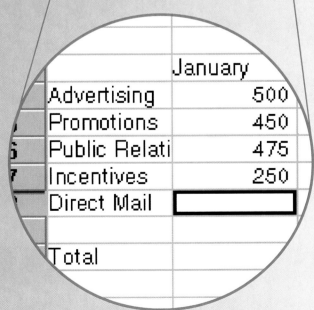

"Why would I do this?"

You can easily erase the contents of a cell by using the Del key. Erasing a cell is useful when you change your mind about the contents after you press Enter to enter the data in the cell. Sometimes you may find that a piece of data you initially typed into a cell is incorrect and needs changing. Instead of editing the cell, you can erase the cell with the Del key and then place new data in the cell.

Task 12: Erasing a Cell

1 Select cell **B8** to make it the current cell. The contents box displays the current entry—the entry you want to erase. The mode indicator displays Ready.

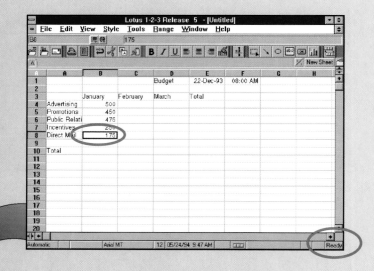

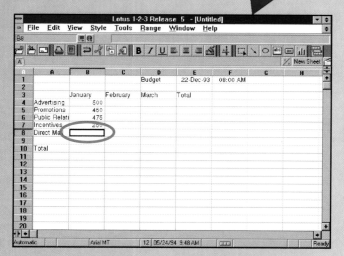

2 Press **Del**. This deletes the entry in the cell.

WHY WORRY?

To restore the deletion, click the **Undo** SmartIcon immediately after erasing the cell.

Copying a Cell

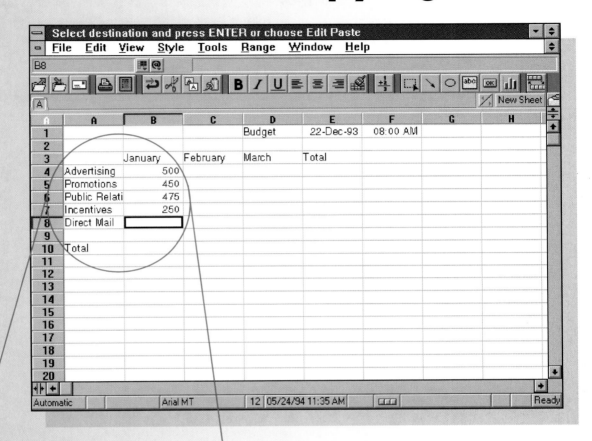

"Why would I do this?"

Instead of retyping information on the worksheet, you can copy a cell over and over again. For example, you may want to copy a number from one cell to another cell. By copying, you won't have to type the number over again, saving you time and keystrokes.

Task 13: Copying a Cell

1 Click cell **B7** to make it the current cell. The contents box displays the current entry—the entry you want to copy. The mode indicator displays Ready.

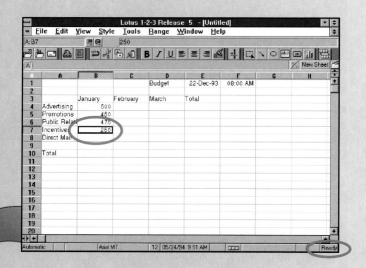

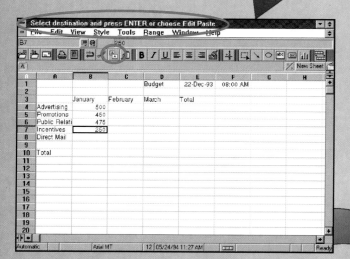

2 Click the **Copy** SmartIcon. The title bar reminds you how to complete the task: Select destination and press ENTER or choose Edit Paste.

WHY WORRY?

If the wrong cell is selected (current) before you press **Enter**, press the **Esc** key and start over.

3 Select cell **B8** to make it the current cell. This cell is where you want the copy to appear.

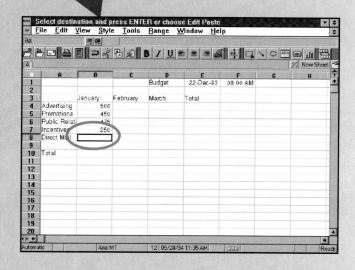

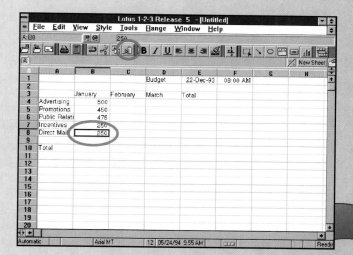

4 Click the **Paste** SmartIcon (or press **Enter**). This step pastes a copy of the data into the cell. As you can see, the entry appears in cell B8.

5 Click any cell. This step deselects cell B8.

WHY WORRY?

To undo the copy, click the **Undo** SmartIcon immediately. Then start over.

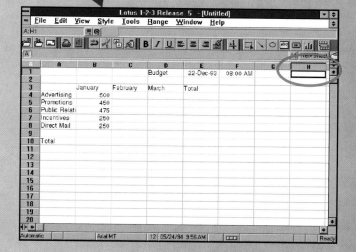

TASK 14
Moving a Cell

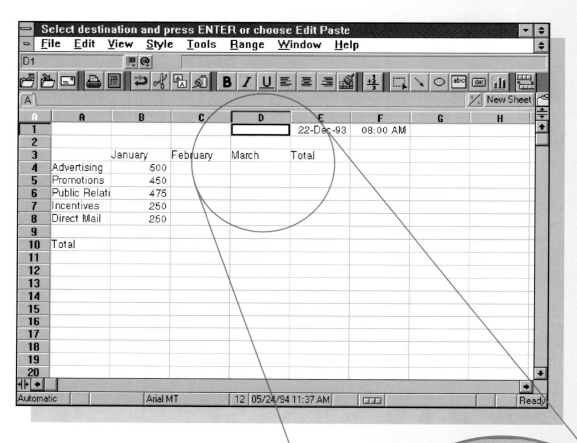

"Why would I do this?"

1-2-3's Move command lets you remove information from one cell and place it into another cell. You do not have to go to each cell and enter the same data and then erase the data in the old location. For example, you may want to move a title that is in the wrong cell, or you may want to move data in a worksheet because the layout of the worksheet has changed.

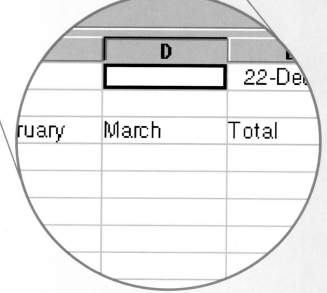

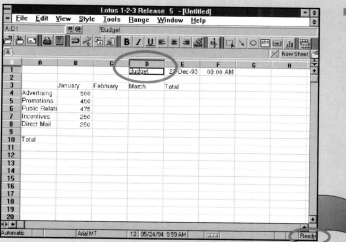

1 Select cell **D1** to make it the current cell. The contents box displays the current entry—the entry you want to move. The mode indicator displays Ready.

2 Click the **Cut** SmartIcon. This step cuts the entry. 1-2-3 removes the data in cell D1. The title bar reminds you how to complete the task: Select destination and press ENTER or choose Edit Paste.

WHY WORRY?

If the wrong cell is selected (current) before you press **Enter**, press the **Esc** key and start over.

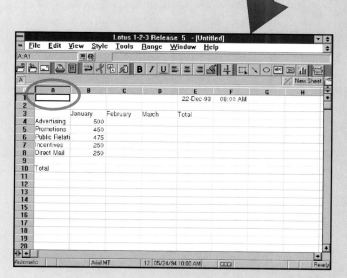

3 Select cell **A1** to make it the current cell. This cell is where you want the entry to appear.

Task 14: Moving a Cell

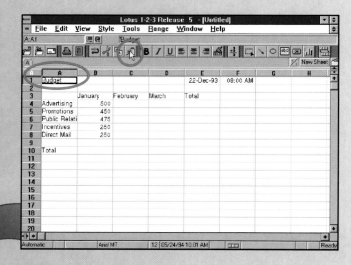

4 Click the **Paste** SmartIcon. This pastes the data into the cell. As you can see, the entry appears in cell A1. Notice that 1-2-3 moves the entry and the format (alignment, protection settings, and so on). See Part V, "Formatting the Worksheet" for more information on these settings.

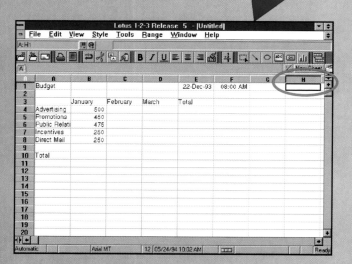

5 Click any cell. This deselects cell A1.

WHY WORRY?

To undo the move, immediately click the **Undo** SmartIcon.

Filling a Range

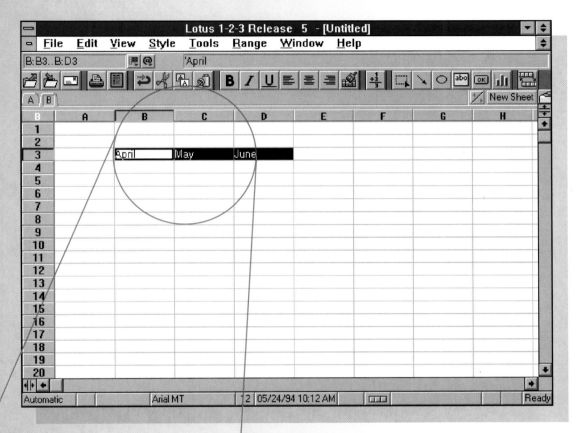

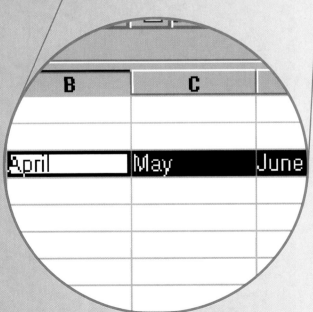

"Why would I do this?"

You can use the Range Fill by Example command to enter a series of numbers or dates. For instance, you can type 100 in the first cell in a range and then you can fill in the rest of the range with the numbers 101, 102, 103, and so on. The Range Fill by Example command is especially useful for entering invoice numbers, checkbook numbers, and ratings.

Task 15: Filling a Range

1 Click the **New Sheet** button to create a new sheet. Then, click cell **B3**. This creates worksheet B and moves this sheet to the top, making it the active sheet. B3 is the current cell where you will enter the first column heading.

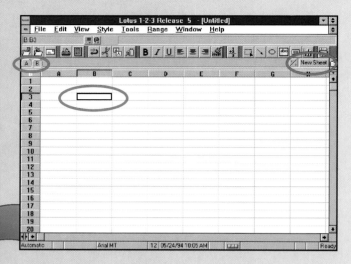

2 Type **April**, and then press **Enter**. This enters the *start value* for the fill and tells 1-2-3 the type of series—in this case, months. 1-2-3 will automatically fill the range based on the data in the first cell in the range.

3 Position the mouse pointer on the lower right corner of cell B3. The pointer changes to an arrow with small horizontal and vertical double arrows.

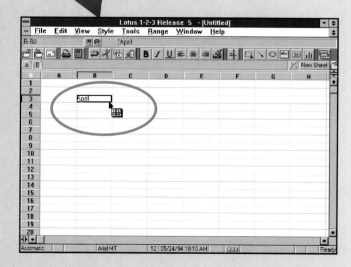

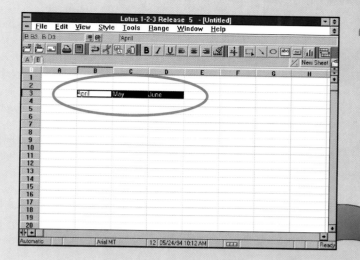

4 Press the left mouse button and drag right to select cells B3 to D3. This selects the range B3...D3—the range you want to fill. When you release the mouse button, 1-2-3 fills the range with months (starting from April and increasing by one month for each cell in the range).

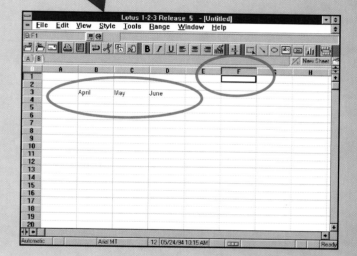

5 Click any cell. This deselects the range.

WHY WORRY?

To Undo the fill, immediately click the **Undo** SmartIcon.

TASK 16

Inserting and Deleting Rows and Columns

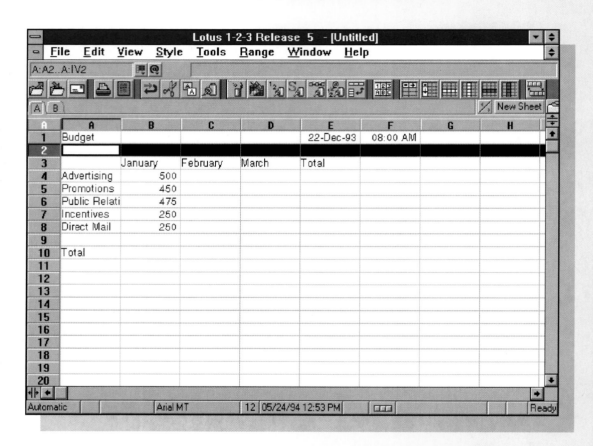

"Why would I do this?"

You can insert extra rows and columns to make more room for additional data or formulas. Adding more space between rows and columns makes the worksheet easier to read. You may want to delete rows or columns from a worksheet to close up some empty space.

Task 16: Inserting and Deleting Rows and Columns

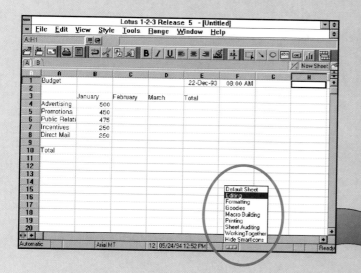

1 Click the palette selector in the status bar and then select the **Editing** palette to display the SmartIcons for inserting and deleting rows and columns.

2 Click worksheet tab **A**. 1-2-3 moves worksheet A to the top, making it the active sheet. Then, click row number **2**. Be sure to click the row number, not a cell in the row. Selecting the row header in a row tells 1-2-3 where you want to insert a new row. 1-2-3 will insert the new row above row 2.

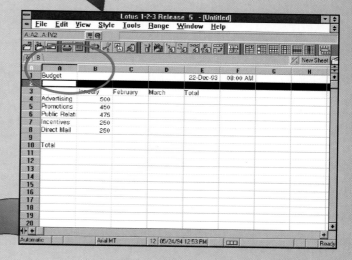

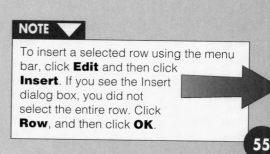

3 Click the **Insert Row** SmartIcon. This selects the Edit Insert command, inserts the new row above row 2, and moves the other rows down. Next, we will delete a column.

NOTE ▼

To insert a selected row using the menu bar, click **Edit** and then click **Insert**. If you see the Insert dialog box, you did not select the entire row. Click **Row**, and then click **OK**.

4 Click the column header at the top of column **B**. Be sure to click the column letter, not a cell in the column. This selects the entire column. Column B is the column you want to delete.

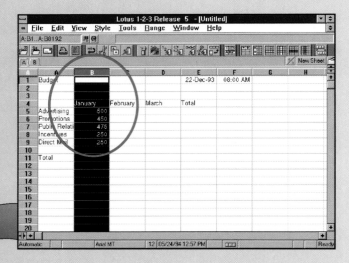

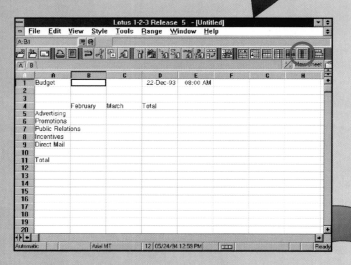

5 Click the **Delete Column** SmartIcon. This selects the Edit Delete command, deletes the column, and shifts all columns to the right of column B to the left.

> **NOTE** ▼
>
> To delete a selected column using the menu bar, click **Edit** and then click **Delete**. If you see the Delete dialog box, you did not select the entire column. Click **Column**, and then click **OK**.

6 Click the **Undo** SmartIcon. This restores the deleted column.

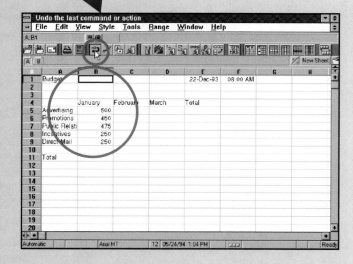

Changing the View

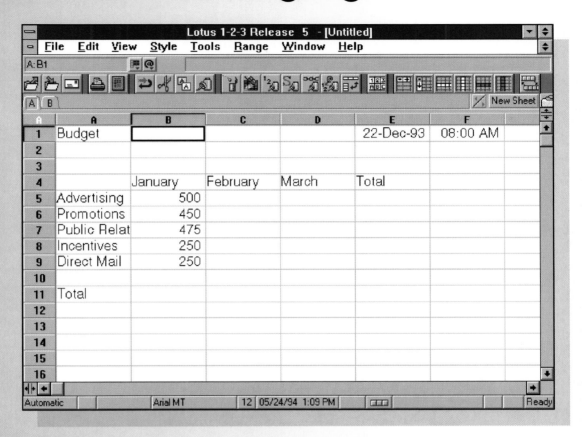

"Why would I do this?"

If you want to zoom in and get a closer look at data in your worksheet, select a higher percentage of magnification. For instance, if you enter a label that appears to overlap the adjacent label, you can inspect this closely without having to preview or print the worksheet. If you want to zoom out so that the whole worksheet shows on-screen, select a lower percentage of magnification.

Task 17: Changing the View

1 Click **View** in the menu bar, and then click **Zoom In**. This enlarges the worksheet by 10 percent.

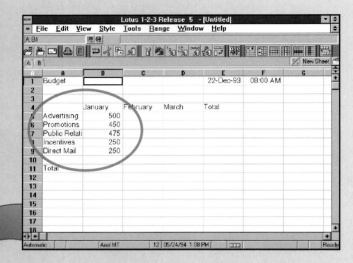

2 Click **View** in the menu bar, and then click **Zoom In** again. This enlarges the worksheet by another 10 percent.

3 Click **View** in the menu bar, and then click **Zoom Out**. This reduces the worksheet by 10 percent.

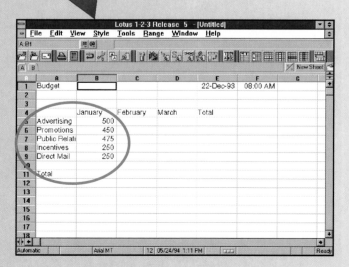

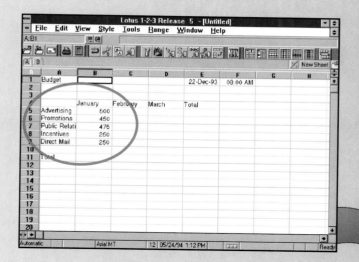

4 Click **View** in the menu bar, and then click **Zoom Out**. This step reduces the worksheet by another 10 percent.

5 Click **View** in the menu bar, and then click **Zoom Out**. This step reduces the worksheet by another 10 percent.

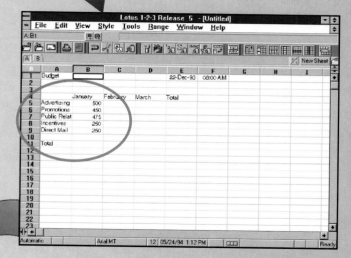

6 Click **View** in the menu bar, and then click **Custom**. As you can see, 1-2-3 redisplays the worksheet at its normal size display. Now you are viewing your worksheet magnified at 87%.

WHY WORRY?

If you don't see the results you want, select the **View Zoom In** or **View Zoom Out** command to switch to the view you want.

Freezing Column and Row Titles

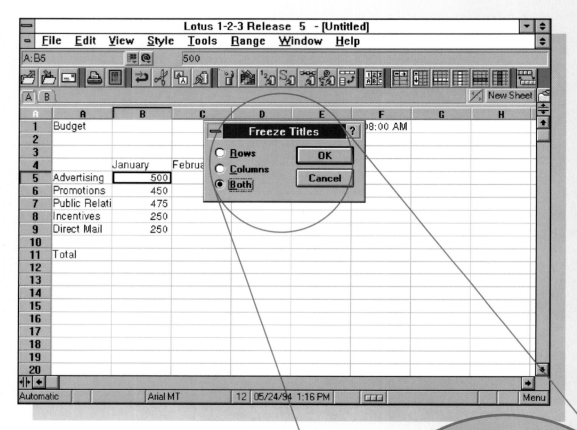

"Why would I do this?"

When you enter data in a worksheet that exceeds more than one screen, you must scroll to the right or down to view all the data. The column titles at the top of the worksheet and the row titles along the left side of the worksheet clarify the data in the columns and rows. You can use 1-2-3's View Freeze Titles command to freeze column and row titles so that they remain stationary when you scroll to other parts of the worksheet.

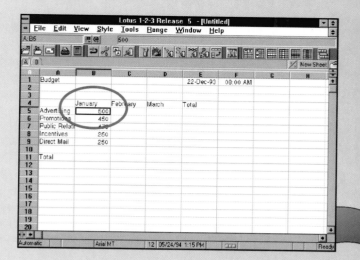

1 Click cell **B5**. Cell B5 is where we want to freeze the titles. All rows above row 5 and all columns to the left of column B will freeze on-screen.

2 Click **View** in the menu bar, and then click **Freeze Titles**. This selects the View Freeze Titles command. You see the Freeze Titles dialog box. The Rows option is selected. We want to freeze both rows and columns titles.

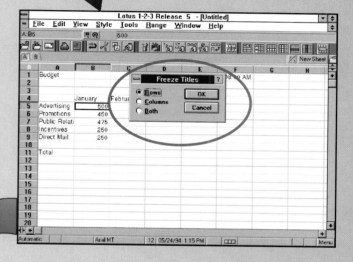

3 Click the **Both** option button. This tells 1-2-3 to freeze the titles both horizontally and vertically.

Task 18: Freezing Column and Row Titles

4 Click **OK** to confirm your choice. 1-2-3 freezes the titles above and to the left of the cell pointer. No lines appear when you freeze the titles.

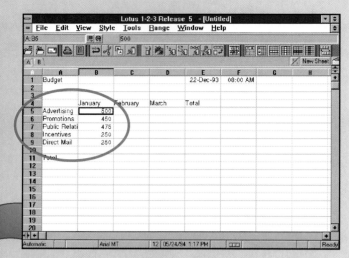

5 Drag the scroll box in the horizontal scroll bar to the far right side of the scroll bar. As you can see, the row titles remain on-screen.

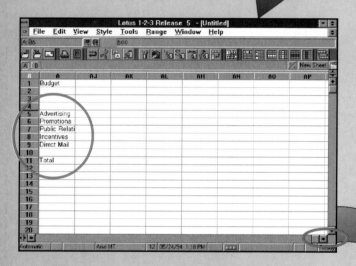

6 Press **Home**. This step returns the cell pointer to the original cell pointer location—cell B5.

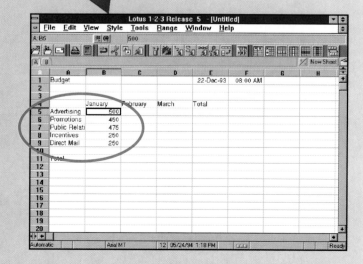

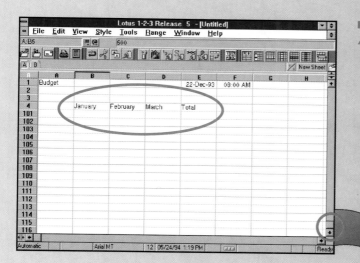

7 Drag the scroll box in the vertical scroll bar down to the bottom of the scroll bar. As you can see, the column titles remain on-screen.

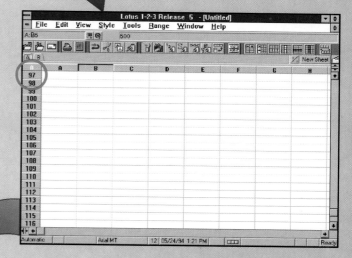

8 Click **View** in the menu bar, and then click **Clear Titles**. The worksheet appears to clear; however, row 97 is at the top of the work area.

9 Press **Home** to move the pointer to cell A1. Notice that the worksheet doesn't look different when you clear the titles.

WHY WORRY?

If you freeze the titles in the wrong place, simply select the **View Clear Titles** command. Then start over.

Hiding and Displaying Columns

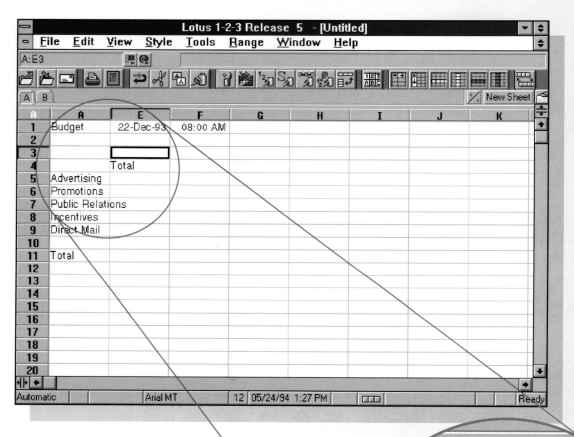

"Why would I do this?"

You can hide columns so that they can't be
seen or printed. This feature is useful if you
work with sensitive data and you do not want
other people to see information on your screen
or printout. When you hide columns, the
formulas that use data in the hidden columns
will continue to work properly.

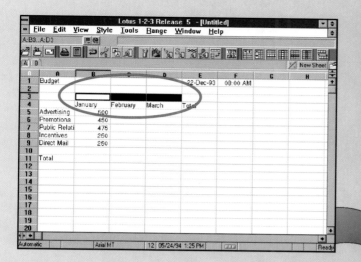

1 Hold down the left mouse button and drag the mouse to select cells **B3**, **C3**, and **D3**. This selects a cell in each column you want to hide—B, C, and D. You can click any cell in the column. (You cannot hide only part of a column.)

2 Click **Style** in the menu bar, and then click **Hide**. This selects the Style Hide command. 1-2-3 opens the Hide dialog box. The Column option is currently selected. The range A:B3..A:D3 appears in the Range text box. This is the range you want to hide.

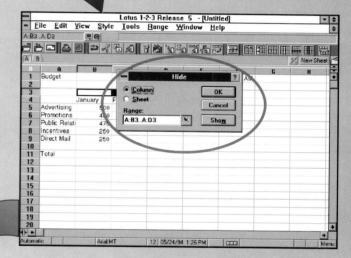

3 Click **OK** to confirm your choice. 1-2-3 hides the selected columns. You can tell by the column letters (A, E, F) that columns B, C, and D are hidden. Next, we will redisplay the hidden columns.

4 Click **Style** in the menu bar, and then click **Hide**. This selects the Style Hide command. 1-2-3 opens the Hide dialog box. The range A:E3 appears in the Range text box.

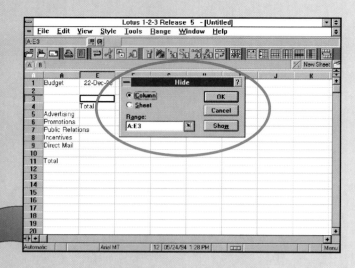

5 Double-click the **Range** text box to highlight the range. Then type **B3..D3**. The range B3..D3 appears in the Range text box. This entry tells 1-2-3 to show columns B, C, and D.

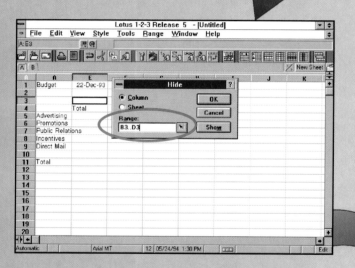

6 Click **Show** to confirm your choice. 1-2-3 redisplays the hidden columns.

WHY WORRY?

To redisplay hidden columns just after you hide them, immediately click the **Undo** SmartIcon.

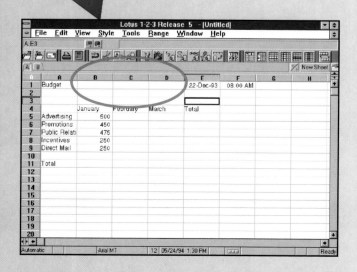

Splitting Worksheets

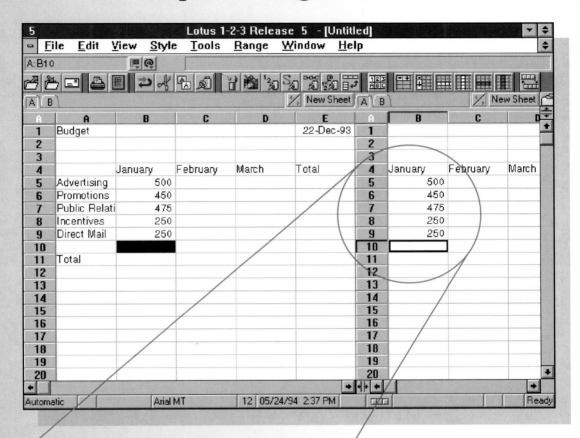

"Why would I do this?"

What if your worksheet contains 100 rows filled with data? As the listing grows, it will become inconvenient to keep scrolling between the bottom and the top. You don't have to worry if you use 1-2-3's View Split command. This feature creates two separate views of the same sheet, letting you scroll to adjust the view in each window. Splitting windows also enables you to compare distant figures side by side. You can split the worksheet horizontally or vertically.

Task 20: Splitting Worksheets

1 Click cell **F10**. F10 is the cell where you want to split the worksheet window.

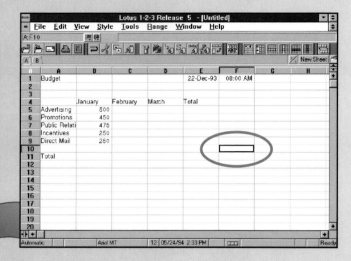

2 Click **View** in the menu bar, and then click **Split**. This step selects the View Split command. 1-2-3 opens the Split dialog box. The Horizontal option is currently selected. This means that 1-2-3 will split the worksheet horizontally, displaying a top and bottom pane. We want to split the worksheet vertically.

3 Click the **Vertical** option button. This step tells 1-2-3 to split the window vertically—in this case, at column F.

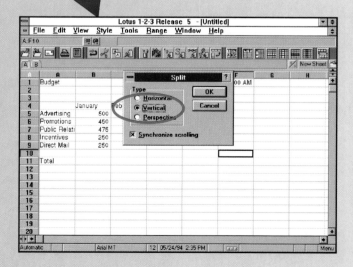

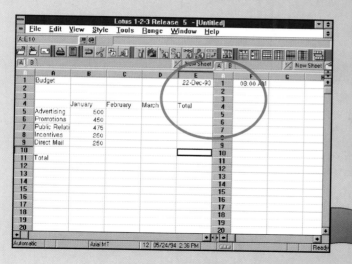

4 Click **OK** to confirm your choice. 1-2-3 splits the worksheet vertically into two panes, a left and a right pane. Notice that a second set of row headers appears between columns E and F.

5 Press **F6**. Pressing the F6 (Window) key moves the cell pointer to the next window. As you can see, the cell pointer appears in the right window.

> **NOTE** ▼
>
> You also can click a cell in the other window to move the cell pointer to that window.

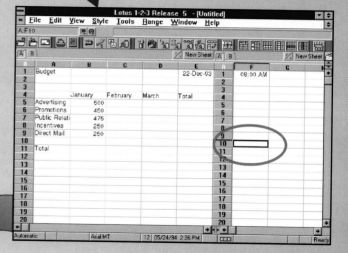

6 Press the left-arrow key (←) four times to scroll. Now you can compare the January figures in the right window to the totals in the left window. (The totals will be entered later in Part III, "Working with Formulas.")

Task 20: Splitting Worksheets

7 Press the right-arrow key (→) twice to scroll. Now you can compare the March total in the right window to the totals in the left window.

NOTE ▼

The cell pointer in the left (inactive) window is highlighted, and the cell pointer in the right (active) window is not highlighted.

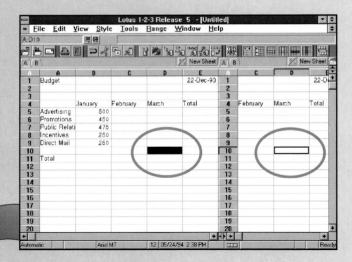

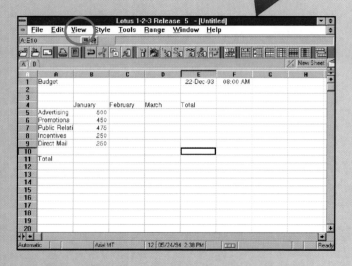

8 Click **View** in the menu bar, and then click **Clear Split**. This restores the window to the original display.

WHY WORRY?

If you split the worksheet in the wrong place, select the **View Clear Split** command. Then start over.

Sorting Data

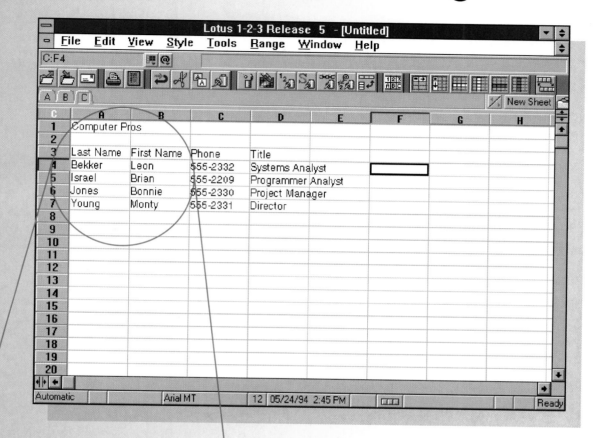

"Why would I do this?"

1-2-3's Sort feature lets you sort text in alphabetical order and numbers in numeric order. The text and numbers can be sorted in ascending (lowest to highest) or descending (highest to lowest) order. You may want to sort a column of row headings so that you can easily look down the sorted column to find the information you want.

Task 21: Sorting Data

1 Click the worksheet tab **B**. This tells 1-2-3 to insert a new sheet after sheet B. Now, click the **New Sheet** button. 1-2-3 creates worksheet C and moves it to the top, making it the active sheet.

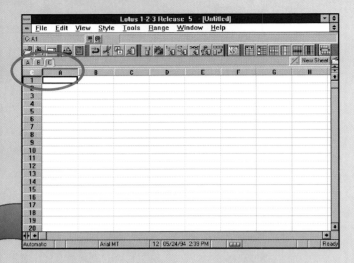

2 Starting in cell **A1**, type the data that appears in the figure so that your computer screen matches the screen in the book.

3 Hold down the left mouse button and drag the mouse to select the range **A4..D7**. Be sure to include the entire range—not just the column you want to sort. If you select just the column, the entries will be mismatched. Also, be sure to select just the data; do not include the column headings.

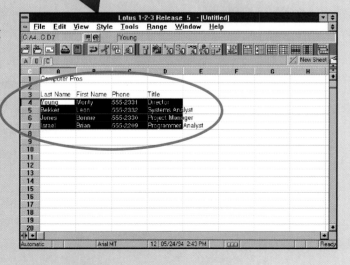

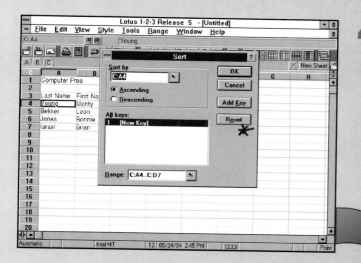

4 Click **Range** in the menu bar, and then click **Sort**. This selects the Range Sort command. 1-2-3 opens the Sort dialog box. The current cell C:A4 appears in the Sort By text box. This entry tells 1-2-3 to sort by column A on sheet C. This is the sort setting we want.

5 Click **OK** to confirm your choice. 1-2-3 sorts the data in alphabetical order according to the last names. Click any cell to deselect the range.

* USE RESET BEFORE:⟩

NOTE ▼

Keep in mind that you can sort by any column, sort more than one column, sort in descending order, and sort numbers.

WHY WORRY?

If the sort does not work as planned, immediately click the **Undo** SmartIcon to restore the range to its original order. Then, click any cell to deselect the range.

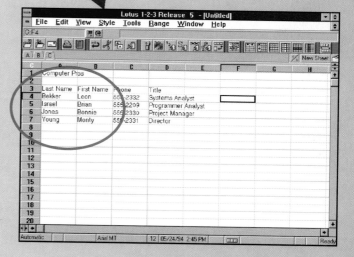

USE RESET BEFORE TRYING NEW SORTING OPERATION
ie. RANGE → SORT → RESET. → C4
THIS WILL SORT IN NUMBERED ORDER.

Finding and Replacing Data

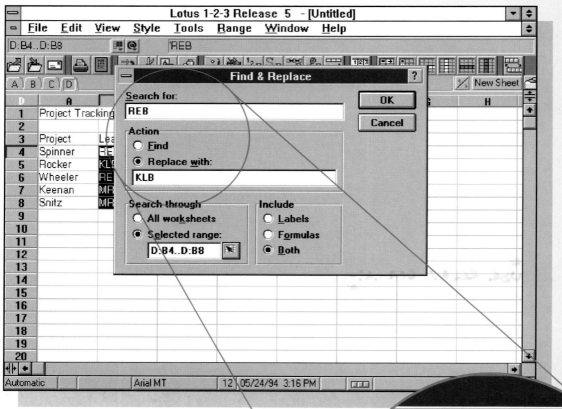

"Why would I do this?"

With 1-2-3's Replace feature, you can locate data and then replace the original data with new data. When a label, value, or formula is entered incorrectly throughout the worksheet, you can use the Replace command to search and replace all occurrences of the incorrect information with the correct data.

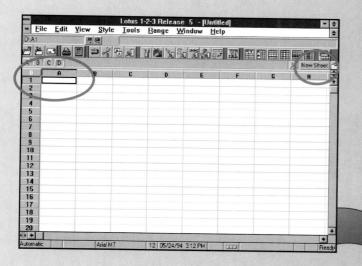

1 Click the **New Sheet** button. This creates sheet D. 1-2-3 moves the sheet to the top, making it the active sheet.

2 Starting in cell **A1**, type the data that appears in the figure so that your computer screen matches the screen in the book.

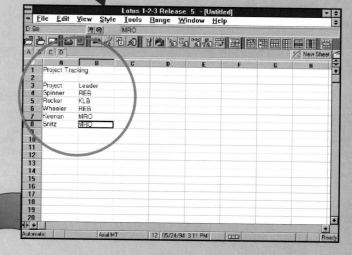

3 Hold down the left mouse button and drag the mouse to select cells **B4** to **B8**. This selects the range B4..B8—the range you want to search.

Task 22: Finding and Replacing Data

4 Click **Edit** in the menu bar, and then click **Find & Replace**. This selects the Edit Find & Replace command. 1-2-3 displays the Find & Replace dialog box. The insertion point is in the Search For text box.

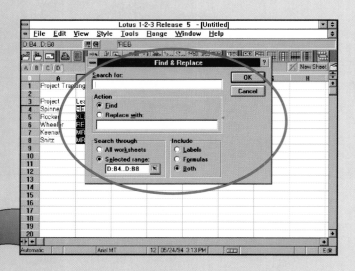

5 Type **REB**. *REB* is the text you want to search and replace.

6 In the Action area, click in the **Replace With** text box, and type **KLB**. This moves the insertion point to the Replace With text box so that you can enter the replacement text. *KLB* is the new label— the label you want to use as the replacement.

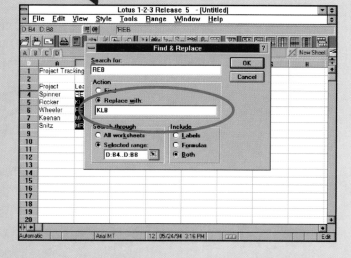

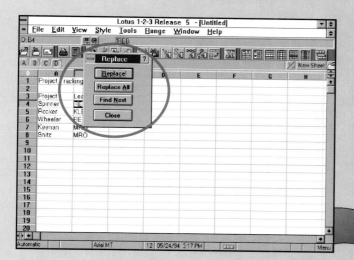

7 Click **OK** to confirm your entries. 1-2-3 opens the Replace dialog box.

8 Click **Replace All**. This step starts the search and tells 1-2-3 to replace all occurrences of *REB* with *KLB*. Then click outside the range to deselect it.

> **NOTE** ▼
>
> If you don't want to replace all occurrences, you can search for and replace one occurrence at a time.

> **WHY WORRY?**
>
> To undo the replacements, click the **Undo** SmartIcon immediately after replacing the data.

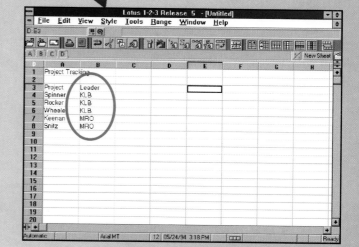

Checking Your Spelling

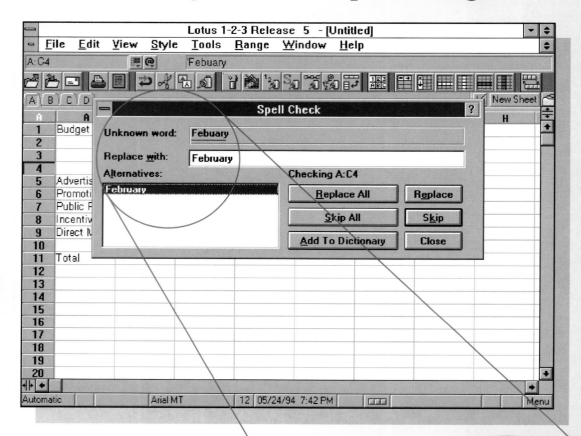

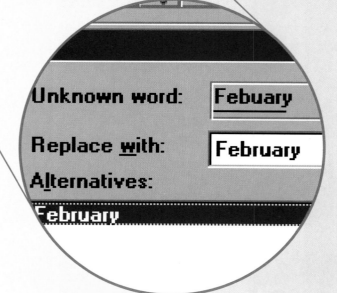

"Why would I do this?"

1-2-3's spell checker rapidly finds and highlights for correction the misspellings in a worksheet. Spell checking is an important feature that makes your worksheets look professional and letter perfect.

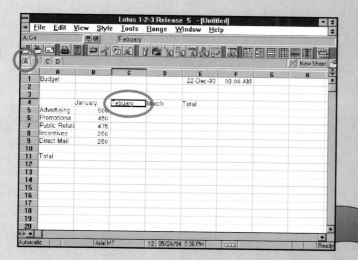

1 Click the worksheet tab **A**. 1-2-3 moves worksheet A to the top, making it the active sheet. In cell **C4**, remove the first occurrence of the letter r in the word *February*.

2 Select cell **A1**. This makes A1 the current cell. This tells 1-2-3 to begin spell checking at the top instead of the middle of the worksheet.

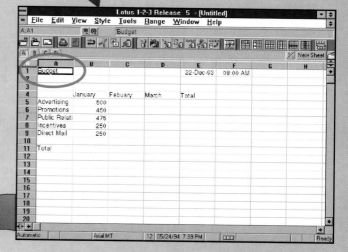

3 Click **Tools** in the menu bar, and then click **Spell Check**. This selects the Tools Spell Check command. You see the Spell Check dialog box. 1-2-3 checks the entire file unless you specify otherwise.

Task 23: Checking Your Spelling

4 Click the **Current Worksheet** option button. This tells 1-2-3 to search only the current worksheet for spelling errors.

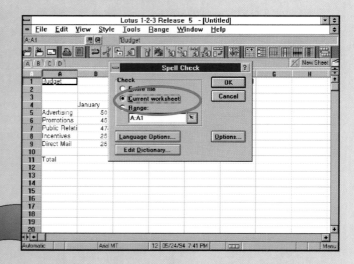

5 Click **OK**. The spell checker starts to search the worksheet for spelling errors. 1-2-3 compares the words in the worksheet to those in its dictionary and flags any unknown words. In this example, the spell checker stops on Febuary and displays a dialog box. The dialog box lists the unknown word and alternative spellings.

6 Click **February** in the Alternatives list. This selects the correct spelling. If the correct spelling isn't listed, you can type it in the Replace With text box.

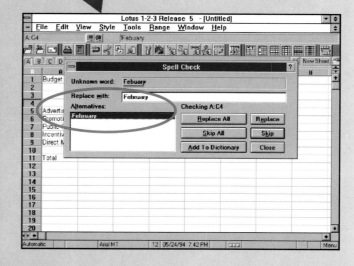

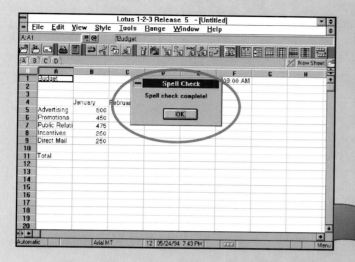

7 Click **Replace**. This replaces the incorrect word with the correct word in the worksheet. The spell checker doesn't find any more misspelled words and displays the prompt Spell check complete!.

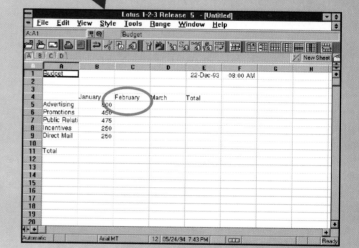

8 Click **OK** to confirm that the spell check is complete. The word February now appears correctly spelled in the worksheet.

NOTE ▼

The Spell Check dialog box covers up the change in the worksheet. You can wait until Spell Check is complete and the dialog box is removed from the screen. Or, you can drag the **Spell Check** dialog box by its title bar to another location on-screen. That way, you will be able to see the changes in the worksheet as they occur.

WHY WORRY?

To cancel the spell check, click **Cancel** in the Spell Check dialog box. Or click **Close** in the Spell Check Unknown Word dialog box.

PART III

Working with Formulas

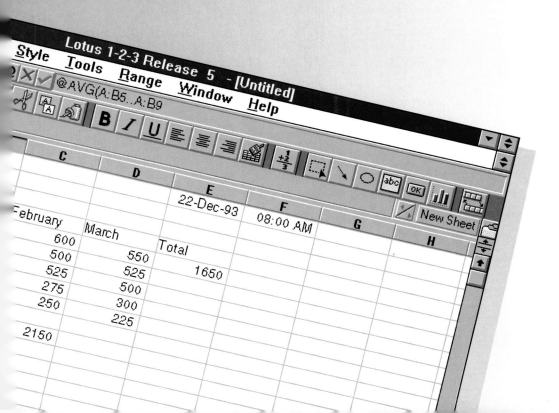

In Part II, you learned how to enter data and change your worksheet data using various editing techniques. This part shows you how to add, subtract, multiply, and divide data with formulas. You also learn how to total cells with the @SUM function, calculate an average, copy a formula, and assign an English name to a range of cells.

@SUM

Formulas are used to calculate the values in other cells of the worksheet. After you enter a formula, you can change the values in the referenced cells, and 1-2-3 will automatically recalculate the formula's value based on the cell changes. You can include any cells in your formula, whether they are adjacent to each other or on separate areas of the worksheet.

Functions are abbreviated formulas that perform a specific operation on a group of values. 1-2-3 provides over 200 functions to help you with tasks such as determining loan payments and calculating investment returns. See your Lotus 1-2-3 Release 5 for Windows documentation for more information.

The @SUM function provides a shortcut for entering an addition formula. SUM is the name of the function that automatically sums entries in a range. In this part, you learn how to use the Sum SmartIcon to create a sum formula.

The @AVG function is a predefined formula that adds the values you specify in a range and then divides the sum by the number of values in the range. You can enter a function like @AVG directly in the worksheet cell, or use the @function selector in the contents box to create a function. For more information, see your Lotus 1-2-3 Release 5 for Windows documentation.

In 1-2-3, there are three types of cell references: relative, absolute, and mixed. The type of cell reference you use in a formula determines how the formula is affected when you copy the formula into a different cell.

The formulas you create in this part contain *relative cell references*. This means when you copy a formula from one cell to another, the cell references in the formula change to reflect the cells at the new location of the formula.

An *absolute cell reference* is an entry in a formula that does not adjust its reference when the formula is copied to a new cell. You can create certain formulas to always refer to one specific cell value. For example, you may want to calculate the interest on several different principal amounts. The interest percentage remains unchanged, or absolute, so the entry in the formula that refers to the interest percentage is designated as an absolute cell reference. The principal amounts change, so they have relative cell reference entries in the formula. When you copy this absolute formula, the interest cell reference will always refer to the one cell that contains the interest percentage.

A *mixed cell reference* is a single cell entry in a formula that contains both a relative and an absolute cell reference. A mixed cell reference is helpful when you need a formula that always refers to the values in a specific column, but the values in the rows must change, and vice versa.

1-2-3's Copy command lets you copy formulas and place them in the appropriate cells. You do not have to go to each cell and enter the same formula. You also can copy the formula from one cell to another cell or to a range of cells. You will learn how to use the Copy and Paste SmartIcons to copy a formula and to drag the mouse to fill a range with a sequence of values.

1-2-3's Range Name command lets you assign an English name to a value or a formula in a single cell or a range of cells. You can then use the assigned name instead of the cell addresses when specifying a cell or range of cells for use in copying, moving, erasing, formatting, or printing.

We will focus on the more basic mathematical formulas you use on a daily basis. The capability of entering formulas in worksheets will show you much of the power and convenience of programs such as 1-2-3.

Adding Data with a Formula

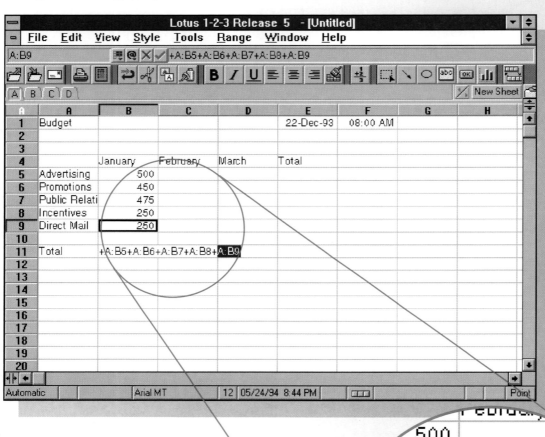

"Why would I do this?"

In an expense report, you may want to enter a formula to sum your expenses. You can also use the @SUM function to add values.

Because a formula references the cells rather than the values, 1-2-3 updates the sum whenever you change the values in the cells.

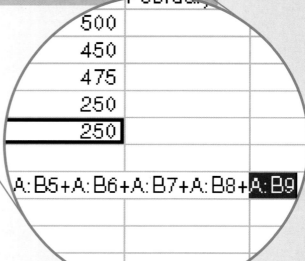

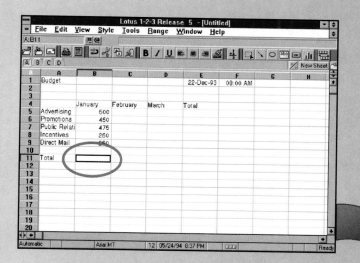

1 Point to cell **B11** and click the left mouse button. This makes B11 the current cell. The answer to the equation will appear in this cell.

2 Type +. This tells 1-2-3 that you want to enter a formula. The mode indicator changes to Value. You select the cells you want to include in this formula.

> **NOTE** ▼
>
> You also can use the arrow keys to point to the cell.

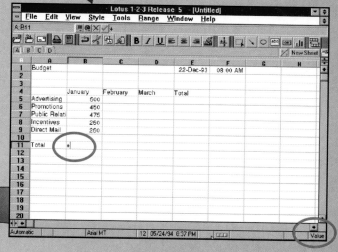

3 Point to cell **B5** and click the left mouse button. This selects cell B5, which is the first cell you want to include in the addition formula. You see +A:B5 in the contents box and in the cell. (The letter A in the cell reference means that the current cell is in worksheet A.) When you have only one sheet, sheet A, the sheet letter does not appear in the cell reference.

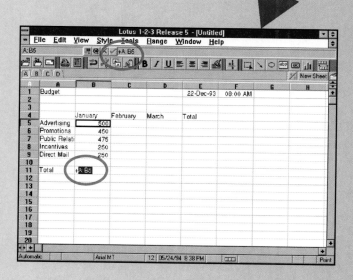

Task 24: Adding Data with a Formula

4 Type +. This time the + sign is the operator. It tells 1-2-3 which mathematical operation you want to perform—in this case, addition. You see +A:B5+ in the contents box and in the cell.

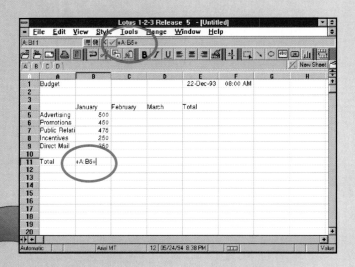

5 Point to cell **B6** and click the left mouse button. This selects B6, the second cell you want to include. You see +A:B5+A:B6 in the contents box and in the cell.

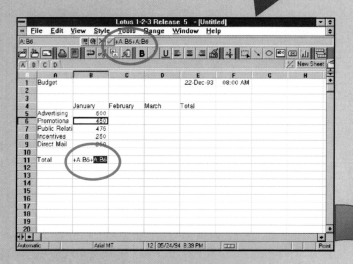

6 Type +. You see +A:B5+A:B6+ in the contents box and in the cell.

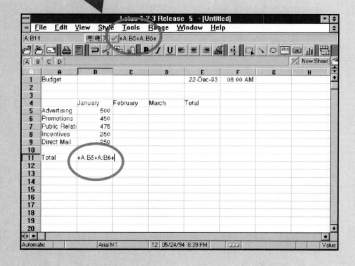

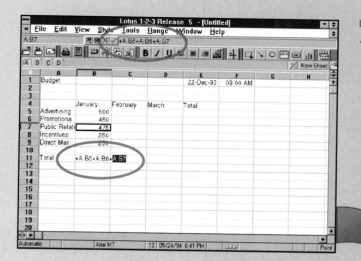

7 Point to cell **B7** and click the left mouse button. This selects B7, the third cell you want to include. You see +A:B5+A:B6+A:B7 in the contents box and in the cell.

8 Type +. You see +A:B5+A:B6+A:B7+ in the contents box and in the cell.

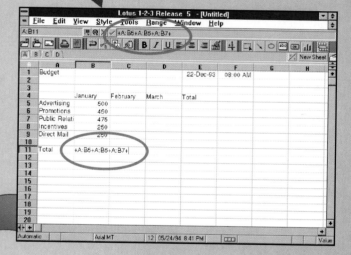

9 Point to cell **B8** and click the left mouse button. This selects B8, the fourth cell you want to include. You see +A:B5+A:B6+A:B7+A:B8 in the contents box and in the cell.

Task 24: Adding Data with a Formula

10 Type +. You see
`+A:B5+A:B6+A:B7+A:B8+`
in the contents box and
in the cell.

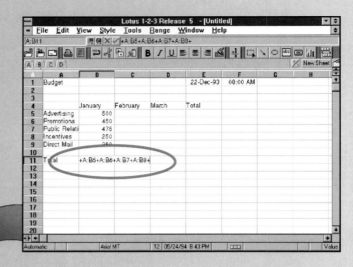

11 Point to cell **B9** and click the left
mouse button. This selects B9, the last
cell you want to include. You see
`+A:B5+A:B6+A:B7+A:B8+A:B9` in the
contents box and in the cell.

12 Press **Enter**. You see the result of the
formula (1925) in cell B11. Whenever
B11 is the current cell, the formula
(+B5+B6+B7+B8+B9) appears in the
contents box. Notice that the sheet
letter reference no longer appears in
the formula.

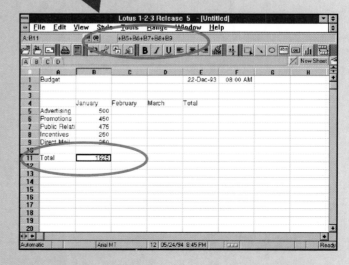

Subtracting Data with a Formula

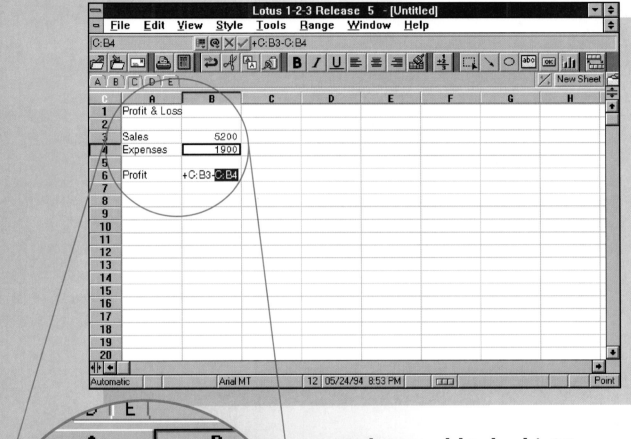

"Why would I do this?"

In the profit and loss statement in the figure, you could just subtract the values in the cells, but if you change any of the values, the result is not current. Because a formula references the cells rather than the values, 1-2-3 updates the result whenever you change the values in the cells. For example, you may want to enter a formula to subtract expenses from sales to calculate profit.

Task 25: Subtracting Data with a Formula

1 Point to worksheet tab **B** and click the left mouse button. This selects worksheet B and tells 1-2-3 where to insert a new sheet—in this case, after sheet B. Click the **New Sheet** button. 1-2-3 inserts a blank sheet, sheet C, and moves this worksheet to the top, making it the active sheet. Starting in cell **A1**, type the data that appears in the figure so that your computer screen matches the screen in the book.

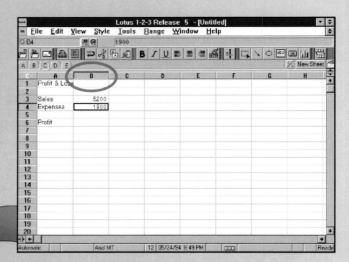

2 Point to cell **B6** and click the left mouse button. This makes B6 the current cell. The answer to the equation will appear in this cell. Type +. This step tells 1-2-3 that you want to enter a formula. The mode indicator changes to Value. You select the cells you want to include in this formula.

3 Point to cell **B3** and click the left mouse button. This selects B3, the first cell you want to include in the formula. You see +C:B3 in the contents box and in the cell. (The letter C means that the current cell is in worksheet C.)

> You also can use the arrow keys to point to the cell.

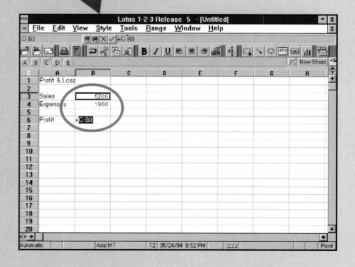

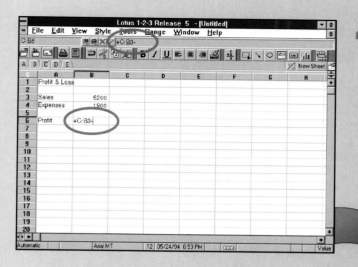

4 Type –. The – sign is the operator. It tells 1-2-3 which mathematical operation you want to perform—in this case, subtraction. You see +C:B3– in the contents box and in the cell.

5 Point to cell **B4** and click the left mouse button. This selects B4, the second cell you want to include. You see +C:B3-C:B4 in the contents box and in the cell.

NOTE ▼

You can include any cells in your subtraction formula. They do not have to be next to each other.

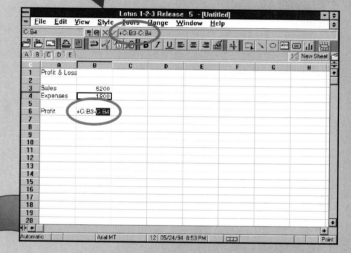

6 Press **Enter**. You see the result of the formula (3300) in cell B6. Whenever B6 is the current cell, the formula (+B3–B4) appears in the contents box. Notice that the sheet letter reference no longer appears in the formula.

NOTE ▼

If you see asterisks (*) in the column, the entry is too large to fit in the column. You must increase the column width.

Multiplying Data with a Formula

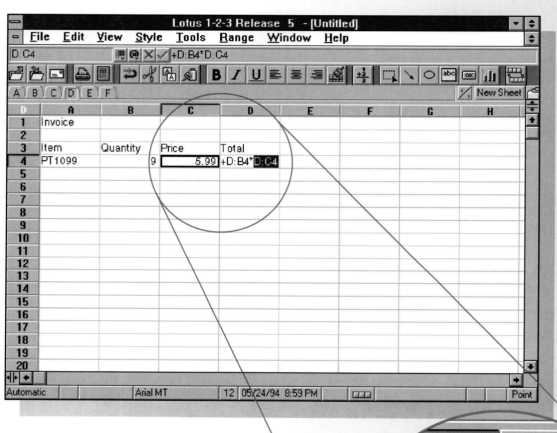

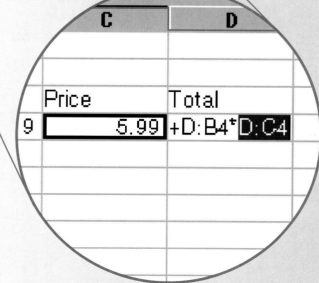

"Why would I do this?"

In the invoice in the figure, you could just multiply the values in the cells (9*5.99), but if you change any of the values, the result is not current. Because a formula references the cells (B4 and C4) rather than the values, 1-2-3 updates the result whenever you change the values in the cells. For example, you may want to enter a formula to multiply the quantity by the price to calculate the total price.

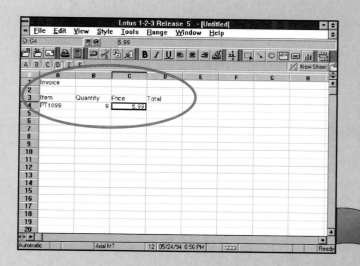

1 With worksheet **C** selected, click the **New Sheet** button. 1-2-3 inserts a blank sheet D and moves this worksheet to the top, making it the active sheet. Starting in cell **A1**, type the data that appears in the figure so that your computer screen matches the screen in the book.

2 Point to cell **D4** and click the left mouse button. This step makes D4 the current cell. This cell is where you want to place the formula. The answer to the equation will appear in this cell. Type +. Typing + tells 1-2-3 that you want to enter a formula. The mode indicator changes to Value. You select the cells you want to include in the formula.

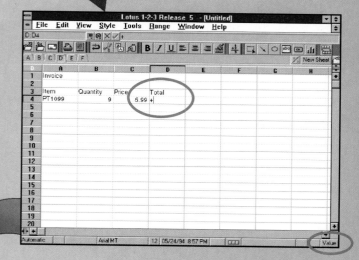

3 Point to cell **B4** and click the left mouse button. This step selects cell B4, the first cell you want to include in the formula. You see +D:B4 in the contents box and in the cell. (The letter D in the cell reference means that the current cell is in worksheet D.)

Task 26: Multiplying Data with a Formula

4 Type *. The * sign is the operator. It tells 1-2-3 which mathematical operation you want to perform—in this case, multiplication. You see +D:B4* in the contents box and in the cell.

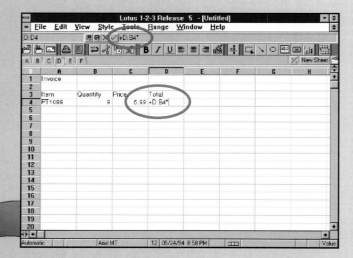

5 Point to cell **C4** and click the left mouse button. This selects cell C4, the second cell you want to include in the formula. You see +D:B4*D:C4 in the contents box and in the current cell.

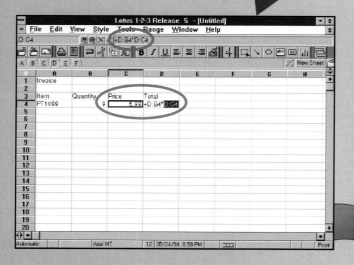

6 Press **Enter**. You see the result of the formula (53.91) in cell D4. Whenever D4 is the current cell, the formula (+B4*C4) appears in the contents box. Notice that the sheet letter reference no longer appears in the formula.

> **NOTE** ▼
>
> If you see asterisks (*) in the column, the entry is too large to fit in the column. You must increase the column width.

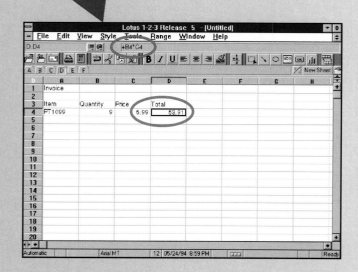

Dividing Data with a Formula

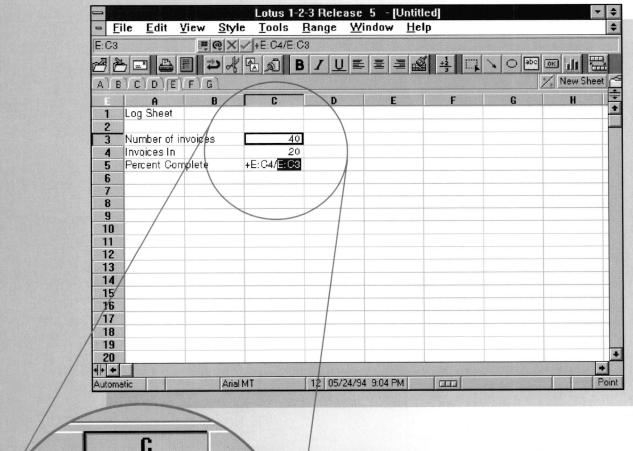

"Why would I do this?"

In the Log Sheet in the figure, you could just divide the values in the cells, but if you change any of the values, the result is not current. Because a formula references the cells rather than the values, 1-2-3 updates the result whenever you change the values in the cells. You may want to enter a division formula to calculate a percentage of the total.

Task 27: Dividing Data with a Formula

1 With worksheet **D** selected, click the **New Sheet** button. 1-2-3 inserts a blank worksheet E and moves this worksheet to the top, making it the active sheet. Starting in cell **A1**, type the data that appears in the figure so that your computer screen matches the screen in the book.

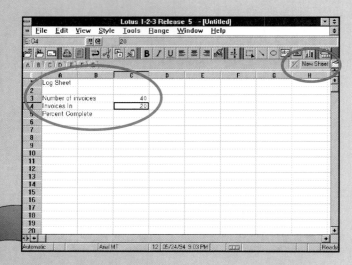

2 Point to cell **C5** and click the left mouse button. This step makes C5 the current cell. This cell is where you want to place the formula. The answer to the equation will appear in this cell. Type +. This tells 1-2-3 that you want to enter a formula. The mode indicator changes to Value. You select the cells you want to include in the formula.

3 Point to cell **C4** and click the left mouse button. This selects cell C4, the first cell you want to include in the formula. You see +E:C4 in the contents box and in the cell. (The letter E in the cell reference means that the current cell is in worksheet E.)

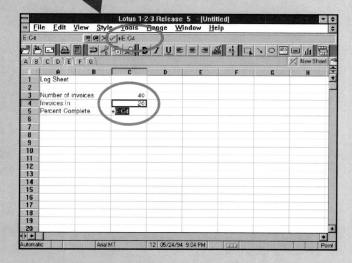

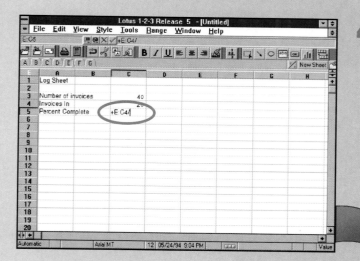

4 Type /. The / sign is the operator. It tells 1-2-3 which mathematical operation you want to perform—in this case, division.

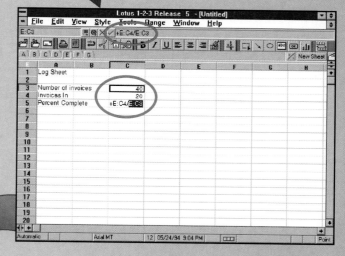

5 Point to cell **C3** and click the left mouse button. This selects cell C3, the second cell you want to include in the formula. You see +E:C4/E:C3 in the contents box and in the cell.

6 Press **Enter**. You see the result of the formula (0.5) in cell C5. Whenever C5 is the current cell, the formula (+C4/C3) appears in the contents box. Notice that the sheet letter reference no longer appears in the formula.

NOTE ▼

If you see asterisks (*) in the column, the entry is too large to fit in the column. You must increase the column width.

Totaling Cells with the @SUM Function

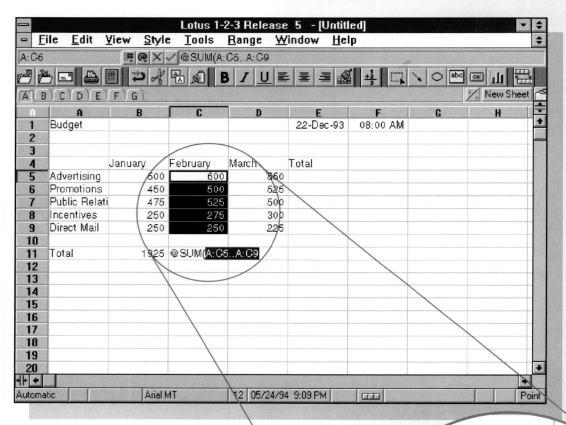

"Why would I do this?"

The @SUM function enables you to sum a range. If you later insert or delete rows (or columns), 1-2-3 automatically updates the total. For example, you can replace a lengthy column or row total formula with a simple @SUM function.

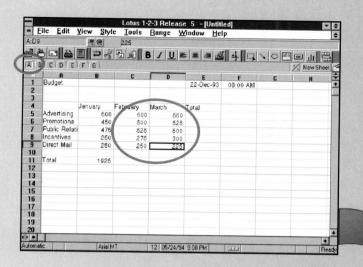

1 Point to worksheet tab **A** and click the left mouse button. This selects worksheet A. 1-2-3 moves this worksheet to the top, making it the active sheet. Starting in cell C5, type the numbers that appear in the figure so that your computer screen matches the screen in the book.

2 Point to cell **C11** and click the left mouse button. This selects C11, the cell where you want to place the @SUM function. Type **@SUM(**. @SUM is the name of the function that automatically sums entries in a range. (You can type the function in lowercase or uppercase letters.) You enter the range within the parentheses.

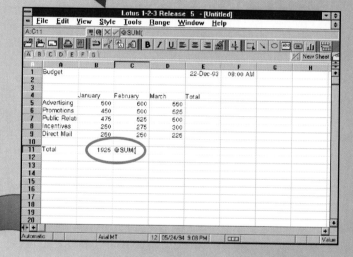

3 Hold down the mouse button and drag the mouse to select cells **C5**, **C6**, **C7**, **C8**, and **C9**. This selects the range you want to sum. The contents box and the cell display @SUM(A:C5..A:C9.

4 Press **Enter**. Pressing Enter confirms the formula and adds the closing parenthesis. You see the results of the function in the cell. @SUM(C5..C9) appears in the contents box. You see the result of the formula (2150) in cell C11.

NOTE ▼

The @SUM function allows you to sum a range. If you later insert or delete rows (or columns) within the range, 1-2-3 automatically updates the total.

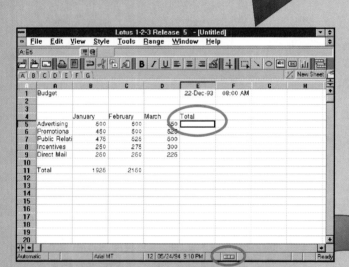

5 Point to cell **E5** and click the left mouse button. This selects E5, the cell where you want to place the @SUM function.

NOTE ▼

For the next step, be sure the Default Sheet palette is displayed (click it in the **SmartIcons** selector in the status bar).

6 Click the Sum SmartIcon. This enters the @SUM function in the contents box and in the cell. @SUM(B5..D5) appears in the contents box. You see the result of the formula (1650) in cell E5.

WHY WORRY?

To undo the formula, click the **Undo** SmartIcon immediately after entering the @SUM function.

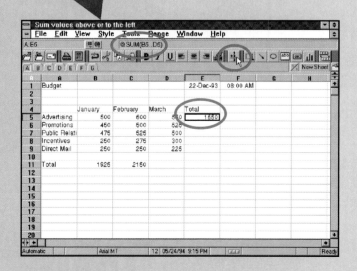

Calculating an Average

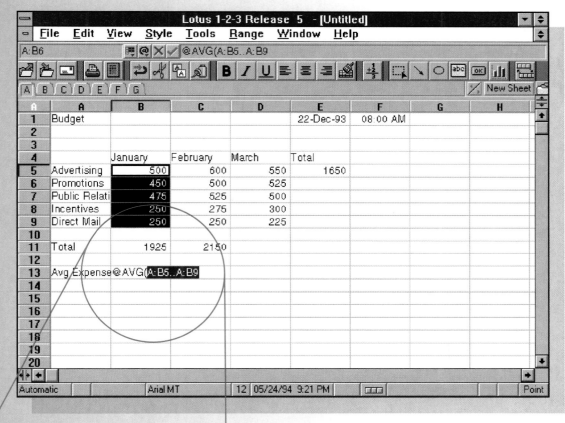

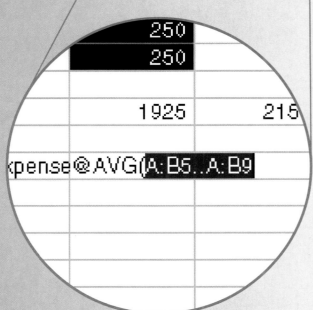

"Why would I do this?"

You can calculate an average by using 1-2-3's @AVG function. The @AVG function is similar to the @SUM function. For example, you can calculate the average expense, income, grade, rating, salary, and so on.

In our budget, let's find the average of the total expenses for January. We will enter the label Avg Expense in cell A13 and the @AVG function in cell B13.

Task 29: Calculating an Average

1 Point to cell **A13** and click the left mouse button. This selects cell A13, the cell where you want to enter the row label.

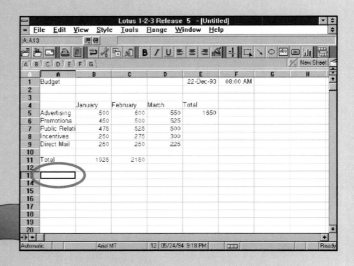

2 Type **Avg Expense** and press the right-arrow key (→). This enters the row label and makes B13 the current cell. B13 is the cell where you want to place the formula that calculates an average.

> **NOTE** ▼
>
> Notice the long label spills into cell B13. You can widen column A to accommodate the long entry.

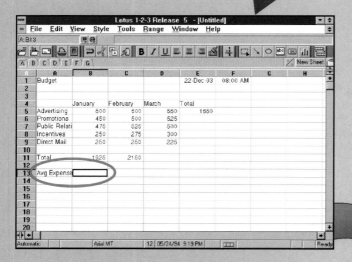

3 Type **@AVG(.** @AVG is the name of the function that automatically averages entries in a range. You enter the range within the parentheses. (You can type the function in uppercase or lowercase letters.)

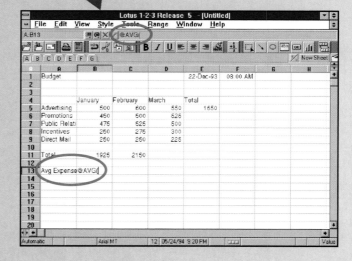

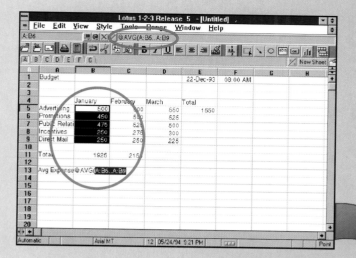

4 Hold down the mouse button and drag the mouse to select cells **B5**, **B6**, **B7**, **B8**, and **B9**. This selects the range B5..B9. In the contents box and in cell B13, you see @AVG(B5..B9.

5 Press **Enter**. Pressing Enter confirms the formula and adds the closing parenthesis. You see the results of the function (385) in the cell. Whenever B13 is the current cell, @AVG(B5..B9) appears in the contents box.

WHY WORRY?

To undo a calculation, click the **Undo** SmartIcon immediately after entering the @AVG function.

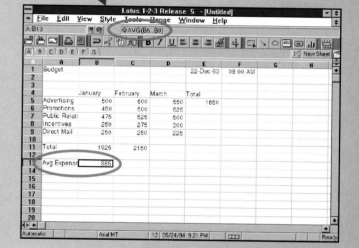

Copying a Formula

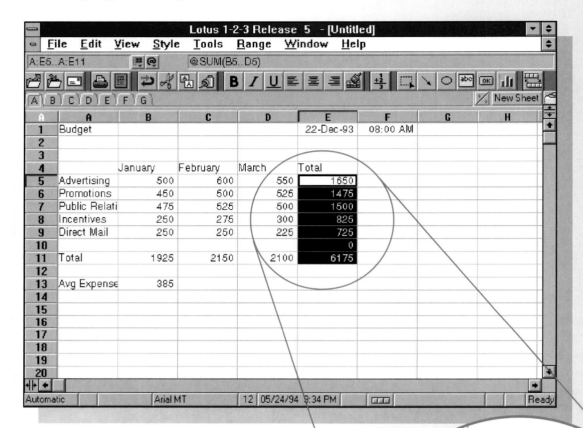

"Why would I do this?"

You will often use the same data and formulas in more than one cell. With 1-2-3's Copy command, you can create the initial data or formula once, and then place copies in the appropriate cells. For example, you may want to copy a formula across a totals row. After you copy the formula, you won't need to type the data to total the row of numbers.

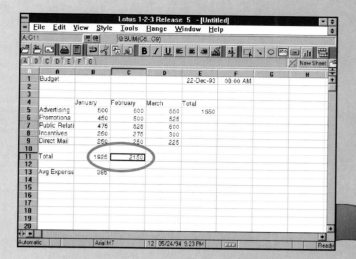

1 Click cell **C11**. C11 contains the formula you want to copy.

2 Click the **Copy** SmartIcon. Clicking the Copy SmartIcon chooses the Edit Copy command. The status bar reminds you how to complete the task: `Select destination and press ENTER or choose Edit Paste.`

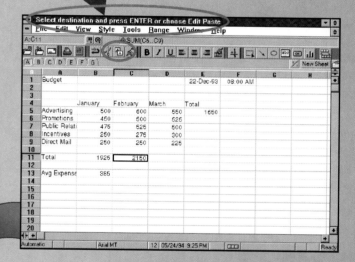

3 Click cell **D11**. This selects cell D11. This cell is where you want the copy to appear.

Task 30: Copying a Formula

4 Click the **Paste** SmartIcon (or press **Enter**). 1-2-3 pastes a copy of the formula into the cell. The result of the formula (2100) appears in cell D11. The contents box contains the formula @SUM(D5..D9). This formula references the current column. This is because of *relative addressing*. 1-2-3 automatically adjusts cell references.

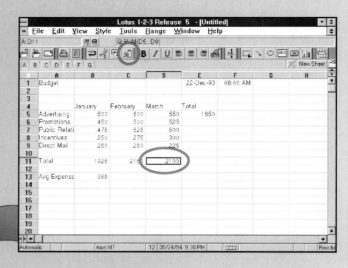

5 Position the mouse pointer on the lower right corner of cell **E5**. The pointer changes to look like an arrow with double horizontal and vertical arrowheads.

6 Press the left mouse button and drag down to select cells **E5** to **E11**—the range that contains the formula you want to copy and the empty cells you want to fill. The results of the copied formulas appear in cells E6, E7, E8, E9, E10, and E11. The formula in cell E10 shows the result as 0. Let's remove the formula in cell E10 because there are no expenses to sum in row 10.

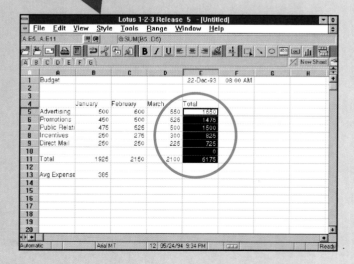

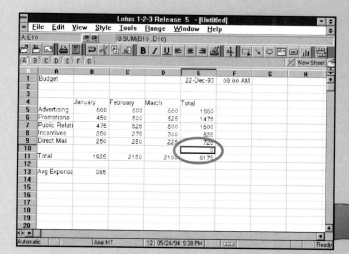

7 Click cell **E10**. This selects E10—the cell you want to erase.

8 Press **Del**. This erases the formula in cell E10.

WHY WORRY?

To undo the Copy, immediately click the **Undo** SmartIcon.

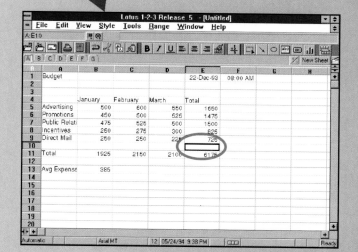

TASK 31

Naming a Range

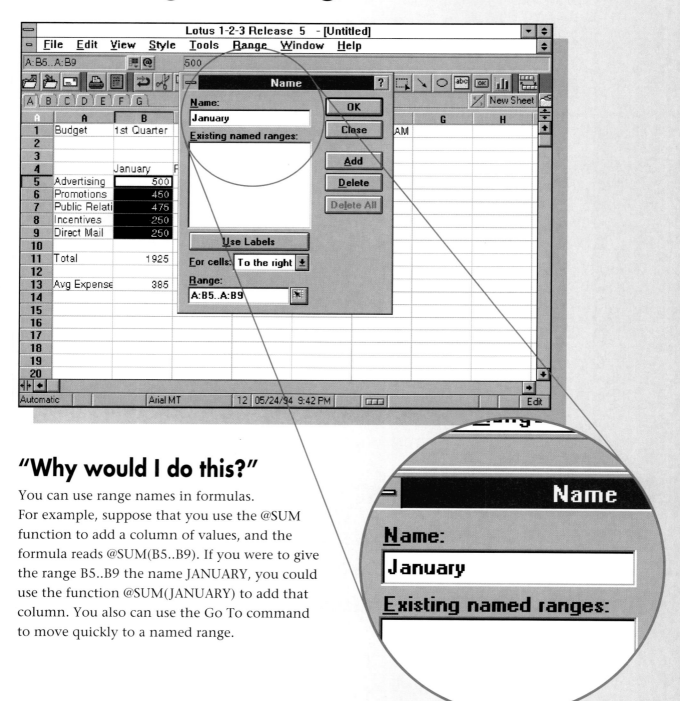

"Why would I do this?"

You can use range names in formulas.
For example, suppose that you use the @SUM
function to add a column of values, and the
formula reads @SUM(B5..B9). If you were to give
the range B5..B9 the name JANUARY, you could
use the function @SUM(JANUARY) to add that
column. You also can use the Go To command
to move quickly to a named range.

110

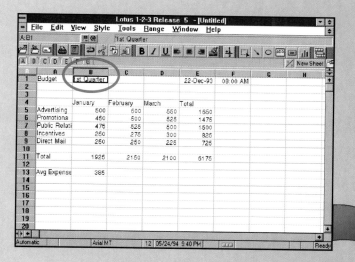

1 Click cell **B1**, type **1st Quarter**, and press **Enter**. This adds the subtitle to the worksheet. Next, we will define a range name for the January values.

2 Point to cell **B5**, and then hold down the mouse button and drag the mouse to select cells **B5**, **B6**, **B7**, **B8**, and **B9**. This step selects the range you want to name—B5..B9.

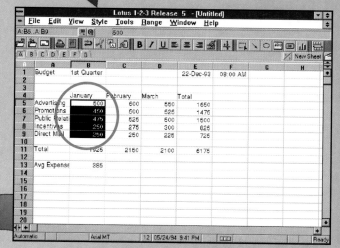

3 Click **Range** in the menu bar. Then, click **Name**. The Name dialog box appears. Type **January** in the Name text box. When entering a name, use only alphanumeric characters—and don't use a name that looks like a cell address.

Task 31: Naming a Range

4 Click **Add**. This chooses the Add command. 1-2-3 adds the name to the list of existing names.

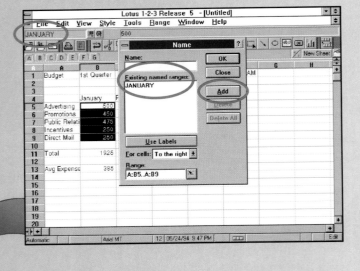

> **NOTE** ▼
>
> The range name **JANUARY** now appears in the selection indicator in place of the range address A:B5..A:B9.

5 Click **OK**. This confirms the range name. The name is saved when you save the worksheet.

> **NOTE** ▼
>
> To delete a range name, choose the **Range Name** command, select the name from the list of range names, click **Delete**, and then click **OK**.

> **WHY WORRY?**
>
> To undo the range name, click the **Undo** SmartIcon immediately after naming the range.

6 Click cell **B11**. This step makes cell B11 the current cell and deselects the named range. Cell B11 is where you will overwrite the addition formula with the @SUM function. Type **@SUM(**. @SUM is the name of the function that automatically sums entries in a range. You enter the range within the parentheses.

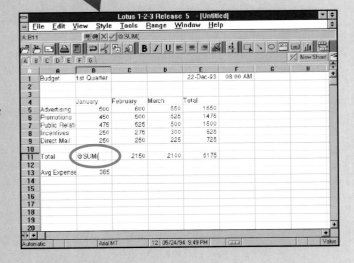

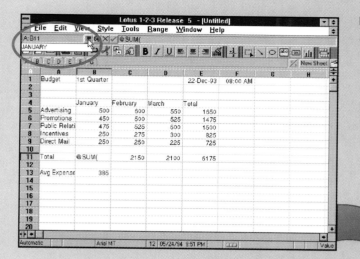

7 Click the **navigator button** located next to the selection indicator. Clicking the navigator button lists the range names created for this worksheet.

NOTE ▼

You also can press the **F3** (Name) key. Pressing F3 lists the range names created for this worksheet.

8 Click **JANUARY**. This selects the range name January in the range name list. The cell and the contents box display @SUM(JANUARY.

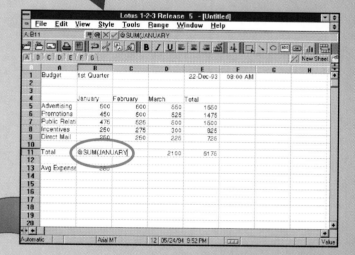

9 Press **Enter**. Pressing Enter confirms the formula and adds the closing parenthesis. You see the results of the function in the cell. @SUM(JANUARY) appears in the contents box. You see the result of the formula (1925) in cell B11.

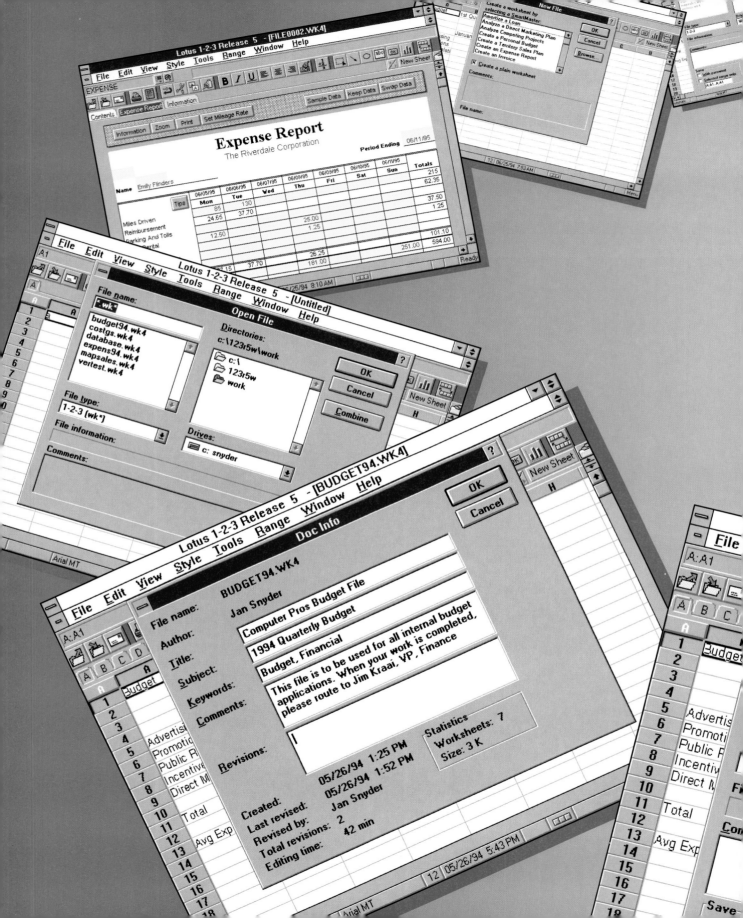

PART IV
Managing Files

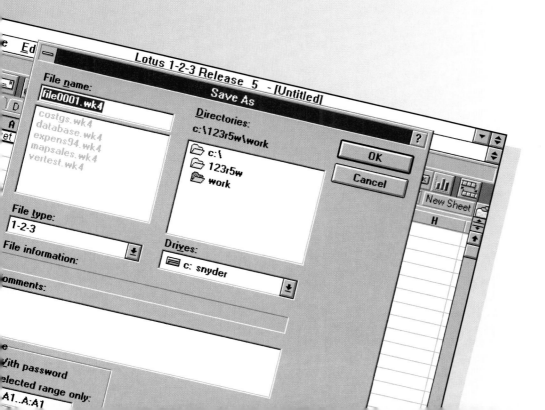

115

Part IV: Managing Files

This part gives you details about managing worksheet files in 1-2-3. You learn how to save your work, close a worksheet, create a new worksheet, use a SmartMaster template, open a worksheet, track document information, rename the sheets, and color the tabs in a worksheet.

Unless you specify saving the file automatically with the Tools User Setup command, 1-2-3 does not automatically save your work, so you should save every 5 or 10 minutes. If you don't save your work, you could lose it. Suppose that you have been working on a worksheet for a few hours and your power goes off unexpectedly—an air conditioning repair man at your office shorts out the power, a thunderstorm hits, or something else causes a power loss. If you haven't saved, you will lose all your hard work. Of course, you should also make backup copies on floppy disks from time to time.

Saving a file on which you previously worked, saved, and then updated is slightly different from saving a newly created worksheet. When you save a worksheet that has already been named, you save the current version on-screen and overwrite the original version on disk. This means you always have the most current version of your file stored on disk.

If you want to keep both versions—the on-screen version and the original—you can use the File Save As command to save the on-screen version with a different name than the original. Saving a file with a new name enables you to keep two separate forms of the same worksheet. You also can save newly named files in a different directory or drive.

Saving a worksheet does not remove it from the screen. To remove a worksheet from the screen, you must close the worksheet. Whether you have saved a worksheet or not, you can close it with the File Close command.

1-2-3 SmartMasters enable you to start a new worksheet with a template instead of a plain worksheet. You can choose from several common business applications and save your own customized versions.

You can open more than one worksheet at a time. For example, you might have two separate worksheets that contain related information. While using one worksheet, you can view the information in another. The number of worksheets you can open depends on the amount of memory available in your computer.

When several worksheets are open at once, they can overlap and "hide" each other—a worksheet can cover another worksheet beneath it. 1-2-3 lets you rearrange the worksheets so that a portion of each worksheet is visible. If you want to display overlapping layers of worksheets, select the Window Cascade command. You can use the Window Tile command to arrange the windows in the tiled effect.

A new 1-2-3 worksheet has one sheet and can contain as many as 256 sheets (depending on your computer's available memory). The first sheet is named A. When you insert new sheets, 1-2-3 names the sheets using the other letters of the alphabet, B through Z, and then double letters AA through IV. You can name individual sheets to identify the contents of each one. For example, you can name sheet A with the name QTR 1, sheet B with the name QTR 2, and so on. You can also add color to any sheet tab.

You can insert as many sheets as you need at any time. This means that you can even add a sheet between existing sheets. For example, you may need to add a new sheet for entering budget data for a new department or for creating a consolidation sheet. As you saw in Part III, you can use the New Sheet button to insert new sheets.

In this part, you are introduced to the essential file management skills that you will need to work with any files in 1-2-3.

Saving and Closing a Worksheet

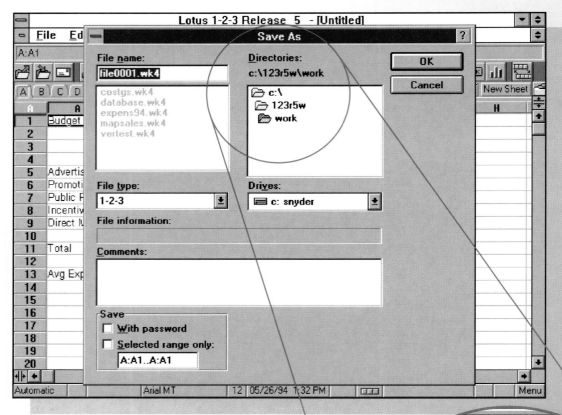

"Why would I do this?"

Until you save the worksheet, your data is not stored on disk. Save the worksheet, and then when you need the worksheet again, you can retrieve it from the disk. When saving files, use only alphanumeric characters in the file name. When you no longer want to work with a worksheet, you can use the File Close command to close the worksheet.

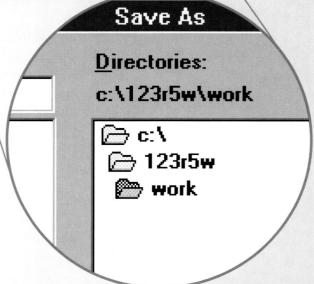

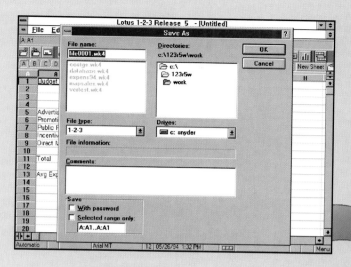

1 Click the **Save** SmartIcon. This step selects the Save command. The first time you save the worksheet, 1-2-3 displays the Save As dialog box. Type **BUDGET94** in the File Name text box. You can type up to eight characters in either upper- or lowercase. 1-2-3 automatically adds the WK4 extension.

NOTE ▼

The Save As dialog box lists current directories and the current drive.

2 Click **OK**. This step accepts the file name and returns you to the worksheet. The file name BUDGET94.WK4 appears in the title bar.

WHY WORRY?

If you type a file name that already exists, 1-2-3 displays an alert box that tells you `File already exists`. Click **Cancel** to return to the Save As dialog box, and then type a new name.

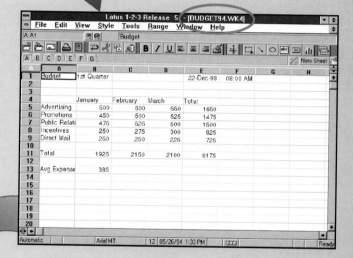

3 Click **File** in the menu bar. This step opens the File menu. You see a list of File commands.

Task 32: Saving and Closing a Worksheet

4 Click **Close**. This step selects the File Close command. 1-2-3 closes the worksheet. You see a blank worksheet. From here, you can open a worksheet or exit 1-2-3.

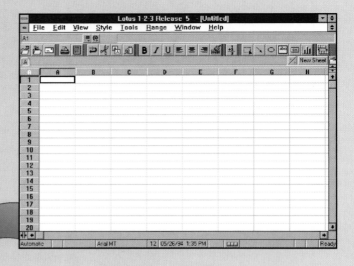

> **NOTE** ▼
>
> You can also use the Control menu box that is located on the left end of the menu bar to close the file. Move the mouse pointer to the Control menu box and double-click it.

5 If you have made changes, 1-2-3 displays an alert box. Choose **Yes** to save the changes and close the worksheet or choose **No** to ignore the changes and close the worksheet.

> **WHY WORRY?**
>
> If you decide that you do need to make changes, click **Cancel** in the alert box. 1-2-3 takes you back to the worksheet.

Creating a New Worksheet

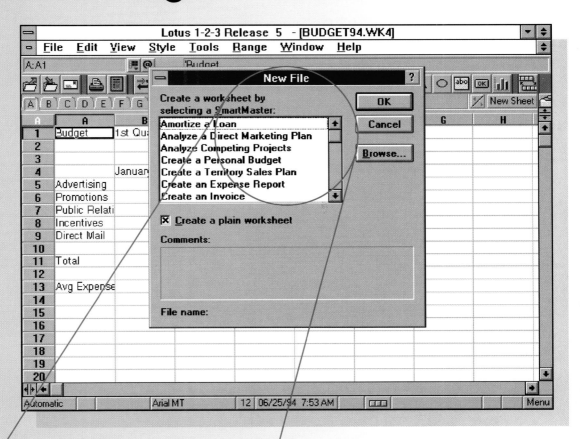

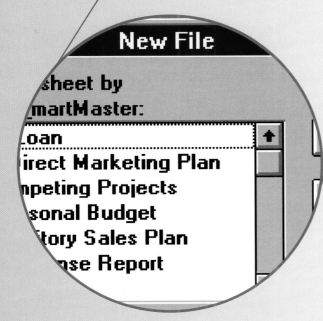

"Why would I do this?"

When you start 1-2-3, the Welcome to 1-2-3 dialog box is presented on top of a blank Untitled worksheet (unless the Welcome has been disabled using Tools User Setup). You can choose Cancel to use that worksheet, or click the Create a new worksheet option to use the New File dialog box. You can also create a new file at any time by using the File New command. Perhaps you have saved and closed the active worksheet and want to begin a new one.

Task 33: Creating a New Worksheet

1 Click **File** in the menu bar and then click **New**. This step opens the New File dialog box.

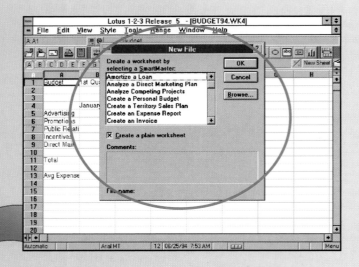

> **NOTE** ▼
>
> You see the options to select a SmartMaster template or to create a plain worksheet. Or, if the Skip New File check box has been selected in Tools User Setup, you skip the New File dialog box; a blank worksheet appears.

2 Click the **Create a plain worksheet** check box (unless the check box already contains an X).

3 Click **OK**. Notice that the worksheet has a default name, such as FILE0001.WK4 in the title bar.

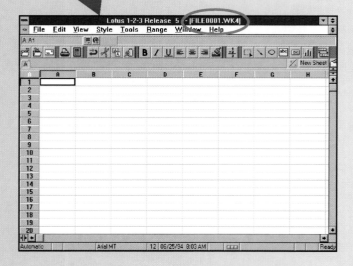

> **WHY WORRY?**
>
> If you don't want to create a new worksheet, *abandon* the worksheet by closing it without saving it.

Using SmartMasters

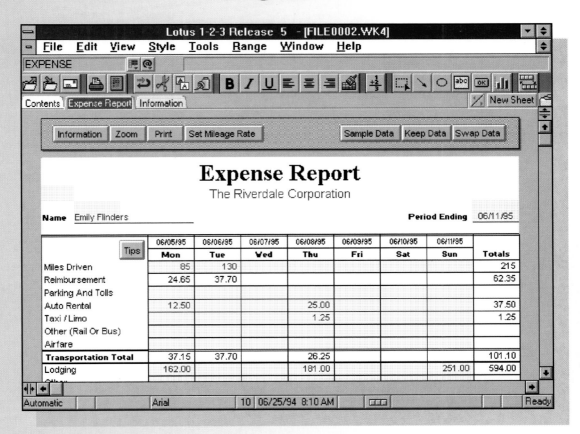

"Why would I do this?"

The 1-2-3 SmartMasters are professionally designed worksheet templates for several common business applications. You can spend less time planning and formatting, yet still achieve very impressive results. You can even modify a SmartMaster and save it as a named template, customized especially for your company's use.

Task 34: Using SmartMasters

1 Click **File** in the menu bar and then click **New**. This step opens the New File dialog box.

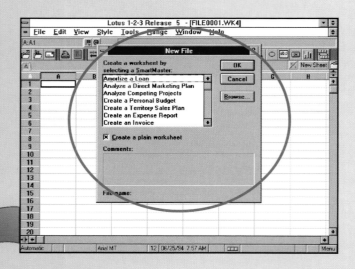

2 Click Create an Expense Report in the list of SmartMasters. Notice the description of the SmartMaster in the Comments box.

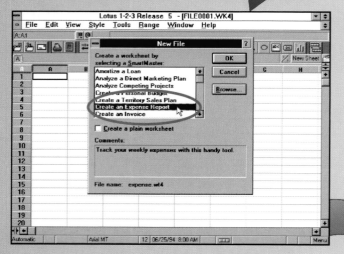

3 Click **OK**. A new worksheet file is created using a default name, such as FILE002.WK4. The worksheet is based on the Expense Report SmartMaster.

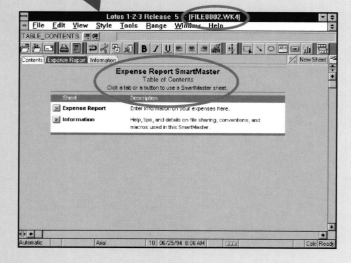

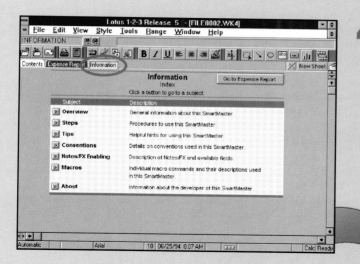

4 Click the **Information** tab (or click the Information button). An index of instructions for using the SmartMaster is presented on this sheet.

NOTE ▼

You can click the various Subject buttons to learn more about this SmartMaster.

5 Click the **Expense Report** tab (or click the Go to Expense Report button). The worksheet portion of the SmartMaster is displayed. You can edit this worksheet as you would any worksheet.

NOTE ▼

The buttons below the tabs give you additional options for working with this worksheet.

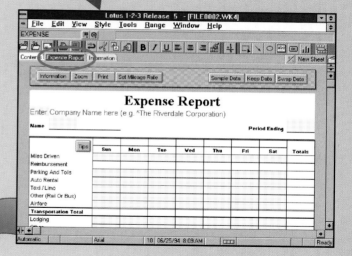

6 Click the **Sample Data** button, and then click **OK** in the message box that appears. The worksheet is filled with data to illustrate its use. Scroll down to see the rest of the report.

NOTE ▼

You can save the file as a template which will then appear in the New File dialog box. SmartMasters and other files saved as templates have a filename extension of WT4.

Opening a Worksheet

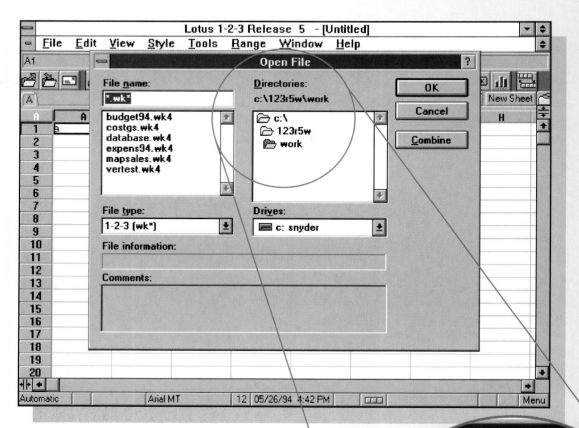

"Why would I do this?"

After you save a worksheet, you can view it
again or make changes to it later. When you
start 1-2-3, you can choose the Work on an
existing worksheet option in the Welcome
dialog box. You then choose the file you want
to use in the Open File dialog box, as described
in this task. Another quick way to open a
recently used file is to click its name at the
bottom of the File menu. If you open more
than one file, you can switch among them by
using the Window menu.

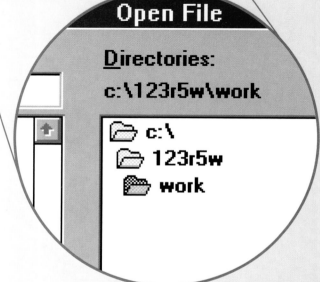

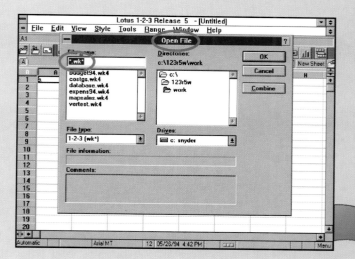

1 Click the **File Open** SmartIcon. You see the Open File dialog box. The text *.wk* appears in the File Name text box.

NOTE ▼

The Open File dialog box also contains the Files list, Directories list, and Drives list. If the file is stored in a different directory, double-click the directory name in the Directories list. If the file is stored in a different drive, click the down arrow next to the Drives list, and then click the appropriate drive letter.

2 If necessary, click the down scroll arrow in the File list to find BUDGET94.WK4. BUDGET94.WK4 is the name of the file you want to open. When you see the file, click the name. The File information box tells you the date and time the file was last revised and the file size.

NOTE ▼

You can type the file name if you know it, or you can use the mouse or the arrow keys to select the file.

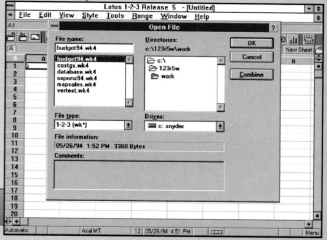

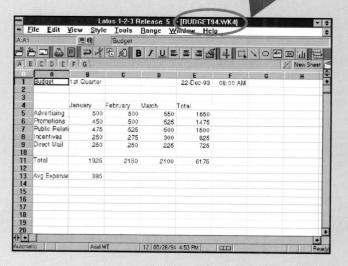

3 Click **OK.** 1-2-3 opens the worksheet. The file name appears in the title bar.

NOTE ▼

You also could have double-clicked the file name, without pausing to look at the file information.

WHY WORRY?

If you open the wrong worksheet, close the worksheet and try again.

Tracking Document Information

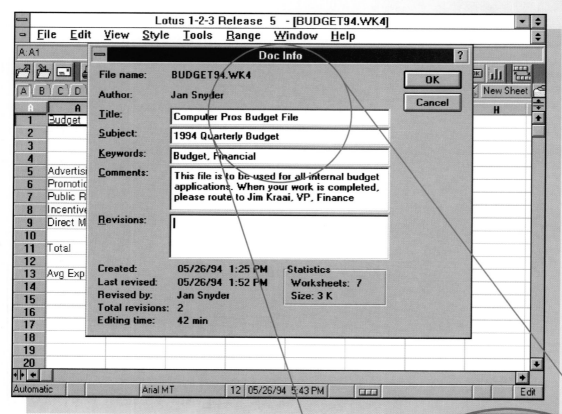

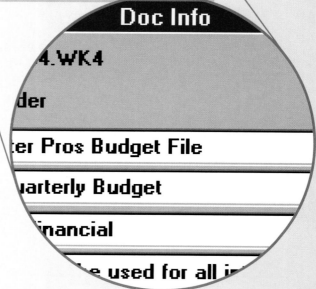

"Why would I do this?"

The Doc Info dialog box allows you to store
additional descriptive information about a file,
including the author's name, revision statistics,
title, subject, and comments. This information
can be useful to others who share the file, such
as users of Lotus Notes. The information can
also be used to remind yourself of revisions you
made to the worksheet.

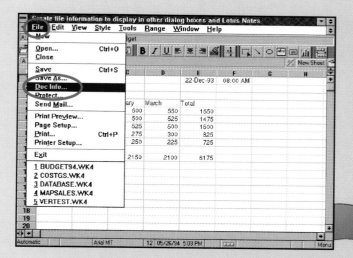

1 Click **File** in the menu bar. This step opens the File menu. You see a list of File commands.

2 Click **Doc Info**. The Doc Info dialog box appears. The File name and Author appear at the top. Other automatic statistics appear at the bottom of the Doc Info dialog box.

NOTE ▼

1-2-3 keeps track of the items in the gray area. You control what is displayed in the text boxes. The author name that appears is derived from the name in the User Setup dialog box, available on the Tools menu.

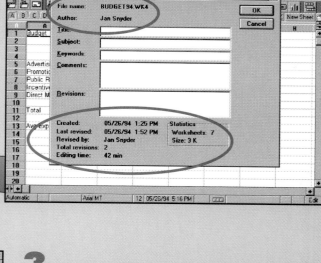

3 Click the **Title** text box. Type **Computer Pros Budget File**.

NOTE ▼

This Doc Info entry is for the entire worksheet, not just the individual active sheet. If you are using several sheets, the Title should be general enough to apply to all.

Task 36: Tracking Document Information

4 Click the **Subject** text box (or press Tab). Type **1994 Quarterly Budget**.

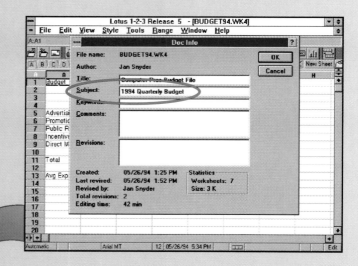

5 Click the **Keywords** text box. Keywords are separated by a comma, and are optional. Type **Budget, Financial**. Continue to enter other information in the **Comments** and **Revisions** text boxes.

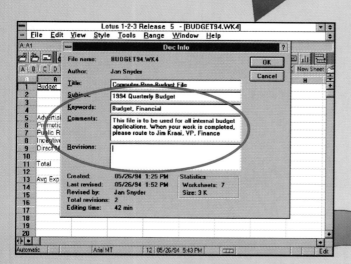

NOTE ▼

Information entered in the Comments text box is also shown in the Open File, Save As, New File, and Save Copy As dialog boxes.

6 Click **OK**. The Doc Info dialog box is closed. Be sure to save the file to retain the Doc Info information you have entered.

WHY WORRY?

If you want to change the comment or other information about a file, choose the **File Doc Info** command again, and then edit the text and save the file.

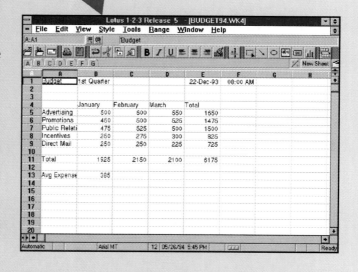

Naming Sheets and Coloring Tabs

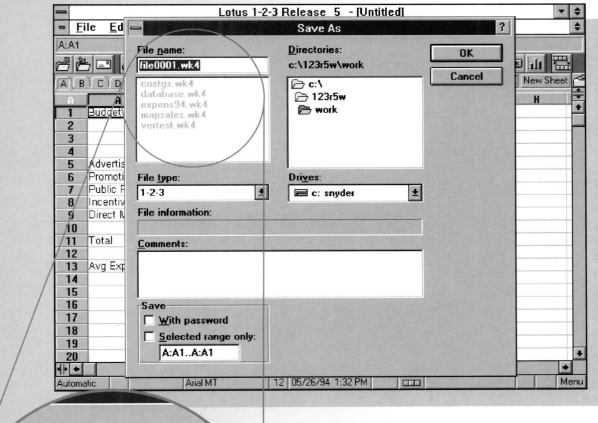

"Why would I do this?"

Naming sheets is especially useful when worksheets contain many sheets. If you want to clearly label sheets, you can name each one individually. For example, if you create an annual budget, you can name each sheet tab with January, February, and so on, and then name the final sheet Summary. To emphasize or color-code the sheets, you can add color to the tabs.

Task 37: Naming Sheets and Coloring Tabs

1 Double-click the sheet **A** tab. Double-clicking the sheet tab widens the tab. Type **QTR 1** and then press **Enter**. The new sheet name appears on the first sheet tab.

NOTE ▼

QTR 1 is the new name for sheet A. As a rule, you can use a maximum of 15 characters, including spaces, for a sheet name.

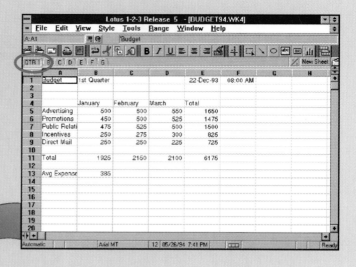

2 Repeat step 1 to name sheet B with **QTR 2**, sheet C with **Profit**, sheet D with **Invoice**, sheet E with **Log**, sheet F with **Phone List**, and sheet G with **Projects**.

NOTE ▼

Adding color to the tabs will further enhance readability.

WHY WORRY?

If you name the wrong tab, just click the Undo SmartIcon to undo the naming operation.

3 Click **Style** in the menu bar. This step opens the Style menu.

NOTE ▼

You also can position the mouse pointer on a tab (for example, the Projects tab), and then click the right mouse button to reveal the shortcut menu.

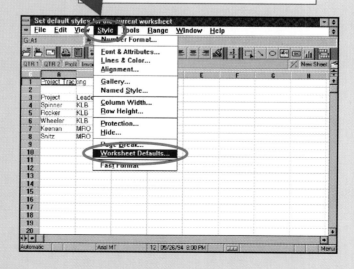

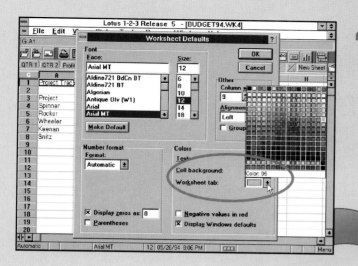

4 Click **Worksheet Defaults**. The Worksheet Defaults dialog box appears. In the Colors area, click the down arrow for the **Worksheet** tab color palette. The color palette pops up.

> **NOTE** ▼
>
> The current color is blinking in the palette. As you see in the palette, the default gray color is called color 95.

5 Click a color to assign to the current sheet tab, and then click OK.

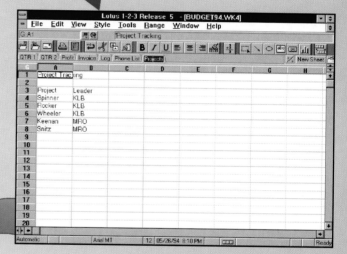

6 Repeat steps 3 through 5 to color each sheet tab. Click the **Save** SmartIcon to save the sheet tab changes with the file.

PART V
Formatting the Worksheet

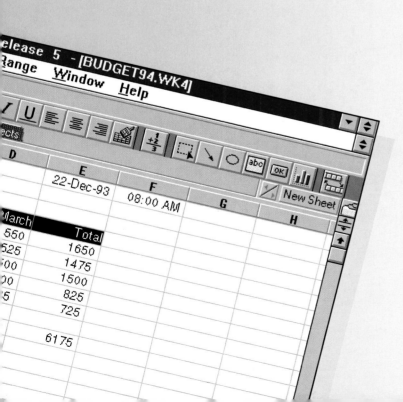

Formatting the worksheet means you can change the appearance of data on your worksheet. With 1-2-3's formatting tools, you can make your worksheet more attractive and readable. In this part, you learn how easy it is to center and right-align data in a cell; display dollar signs, commas, and percent signs; change the number of decimal places; and format a date and time. You also learn how to change column width, format individual words, use style templates, copy styles, shade cells, add borders, and hide grid lines.

You can align data in a cell left, center, or right. The default alignment is General. *General alignment* means that numbers are right-aligned and text is left-aligned.

The default number format is Automatic. The *Automatic number format* means that 1-2-3 automatically formats numbers, dates, and times, depending on how you enter the data. For example, if you enter a number with a dollar sign, 1-2-3 automatically formats the number as US Dollar. You can format cells that don't contain numbers yet. When you enter numbers into the cells, the numbers automatically appear formatted.

1-2-3 lets you change the width of any column and the height of any row. You can quickly change the width of any column by double-clicking the line next to the column letter in the column you want to adjust. 1-2-3 automatically changes the width of the column based on the longest entry in that column.

A *font* is a style of type in a particular typeface and size. 1-2-3 displays various fonts and font sizes in the status bar. You can use the fonts provided by 1-2-3 as well as fonts designed especially for your printer.

You can apply fonts to a single cell or a range of cells. You can also change the font size, font style, and font colors. Font styles include bold, italic, and underline. The Color option in the Font & Attributes dialog box lets you change font colors. Varying the font colors to emphasize data makes your worksheet more attractive. Of course, you must have a color monitor and a color printer to benefit from changing font colors.

After you set the format of a cell or range of cells, you can choose to copy only the format—the style but not the contents—to another cell or range of cells. 1-2-3's Edit Copy and Edit Paste Special commands let you copy formats.

You can also add shading to your worksheet to draw attention to words and numbers you want to emphasize. You can shade cells with a light dot pattern, diagonal lines, or choose from many other types of patterns.

Italic

One of the best ways to enhance the appearance of a worksheet is to add borders to the data on the worksheet. You can use the Style Lines & Color command to add boxes around cells and ranges, and you can add emphasis lines anywhere on the worksheet.

In 1-2-3, you can apply preset formats to selected data on a worksheet with the Style Gallery command. Generally, you apply one format at a time to a selected range. However, now you can apply a collection of formats, or a *style*, which are supplied by 1-2-3 all at once. The formats help you create professional-looking financial reports, lists, and large tables.

Another way to change the overall worksheet display is to remove the grid lines that separate the cells in the worksheet. Your worksheet looks cleaner when you hide the grid lines. Removing grid lines doesn't affect the printed version of the worksheet.

In this part, you learn some of the most important formatting operations for changing the appearance and layout of your worksheets.

Underline

TASK 38

Aligning Data

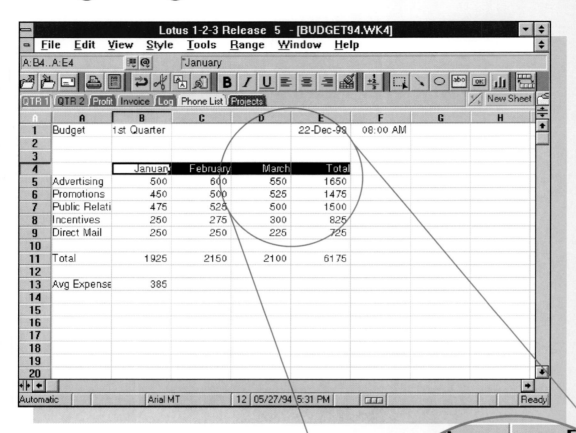

"Why would I do this?"

When you enter data into a cell, numbers, dates, and times automatically align with the right side of the cell. Text aligns with the left side of the cell. You can change the alignment of information at any time. For instance, you may want to fine-tune the appearance of column headings across columns. You can right-align column headings across the columns to line up the headings with the numbers that are right-aligned.

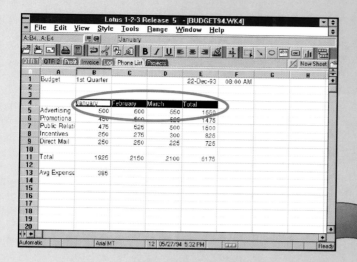

1 Hold down the mouse button and drag the mouse to select cells **B4**, **C4**, **D4**, and **E4**. This selects the range you want to right-align—B4..E4. Notice that these entries are left-aligned.

NOTE ▼

In Release 5 of 1-2-3 for Windows, you do *not* need to keep numbers right-aligned to use the numbers in a formula. Even a mixture of alignments in a range of numbers will calculate correctly.

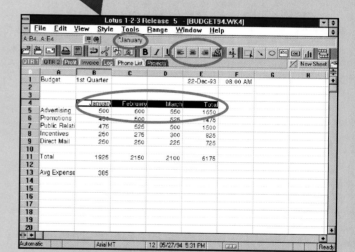

2 Click the **Right Align** SmartIcon. Then, click any cell to deselect the range. 1-2-3 right-aligns the contents of each cell in the range. Because the entries are text, an alignment prefix (") is added to each entry in the contents box.

NOTE ▼

If you center-align, the ^ prefix appears before the entry in the contents box. Left-aligned entries have an ' (apostrophe) prefix.

WHY WORRY?

To undo the most recent alignment change, click the **Undo** SmartIcon.

Displaying Dollar Signs, Commas, and Percent Signs

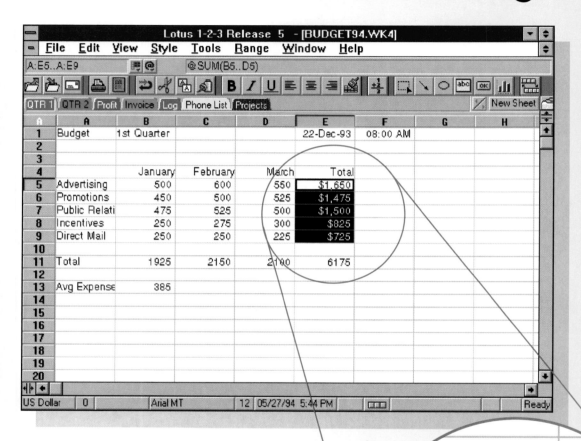

"Why would I do this?"

With 1-2-3's Number Format command, you can display numeric values in many ways. *Formatting* a number means changing the way it is displayed. For instance, you can format the number 600 to look like currency, $600.00. It is important that the numbers in your worksheet appear in the correct format.

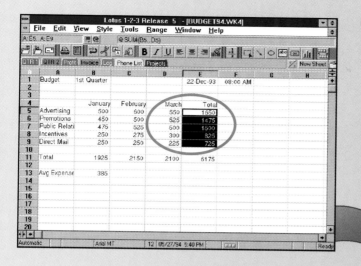

1 Hold down the mouse button and drag the mouse to select cells **E5**, **E6**, **E7**, **E8**, and **E9**. This selects the range E5..E9 in which you want to display dollar signs.

2 Click the **format selector** on the status bar. This displays a list of number formats. The format selector is the first panel and usually displays Automatic.

NOTE ▼

You can also click the selected range with the right mouse button. 1-2-3 displays the quick menu. Then, choose **Number Format.**

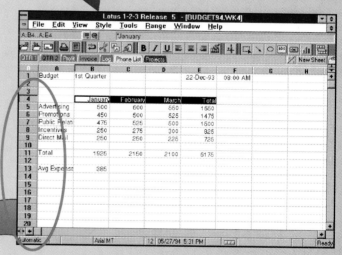

3 Click **US Dollar**. Then, click any cell to deselect the range. Clicking US Dollar tells 1-2-3 to display dollar signs, commas, and two decimal places. Notice that the status bar displays the new format—US Dollar and 2.

4 Click the **decimal selector** on the status bar. This displays a list of decimal places from 0 to 15. The decimal selector is the second panel. In the figure, the decimal selector displays 2.

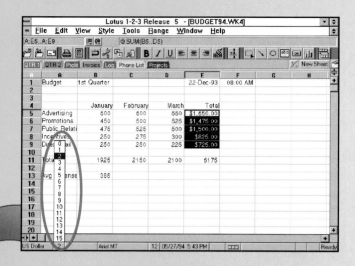

5 Click **0**. Then, click any cell to deselect the range. Clicking 0 tells 1-2-3 to display zero decimal places. Notice that the status bar displays the new format—**0**.

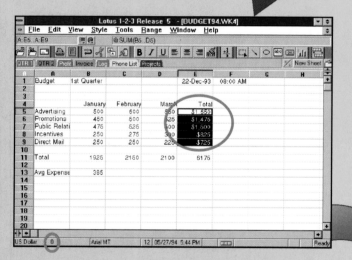

NOTE ▼

If you select zero decimal places, 1-2-3 rounds the values to fit this format. However, the actual values will be used in calculations.

6 Click the **Log** sheet tab to move to the log worksheet. Then, click cell **C5**. This selects cell C5 in which you want to display a percent sign.

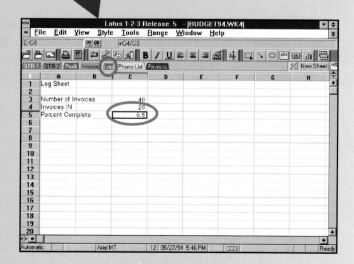

Task 39: Displaying Dollar Signs, Commas, and Percent Signs

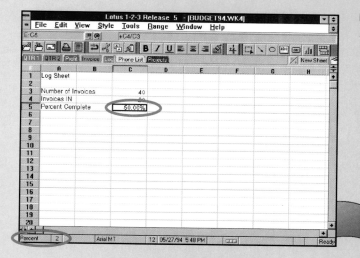

7 Click the **format selector** on the status bar to display a list of number formats. Click **Percent**. Clicking Percent tells 1-2-3 to display percent signs and two decimal places. Notice that the status bar displays the new format—Percent and 2.

NOTE ▼

If you see asterisks (*) in the column, the entry is too long to fit. You must increase the column width.

8 Click the **decimal selector** on the status bar to display a list of decimal place numbers. Click **0**. Clicking 0 tells 1-2-3 to display zero decimal places. Notice that the status bar displays the new format—0.

WHY WORRY?

To undo the most recent formatting change, click the **Undo** SmartIcon.

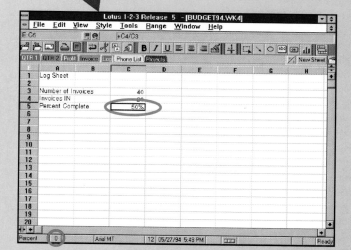

Changing Date and Time Formats

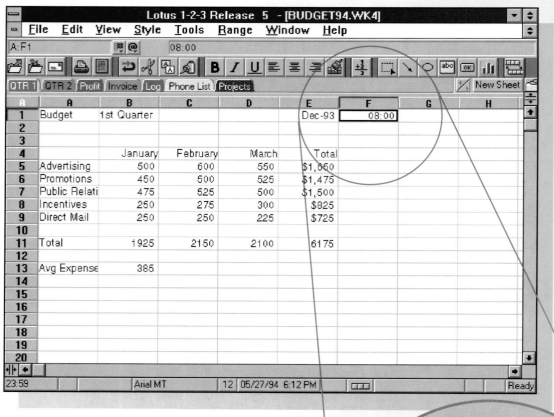

"Why would I do this?"

In 1-2-3, you can enter dates in several different ways so that 1-2-3 accepts the date and display in a particular format. If you like, you can change the way 1-2-3 displays the date and the time. For instance, Jun-94 may be clearer than 6/1/94. 1-2-3 assumes the 24-hour time format unless you enter an AM or PM designation.

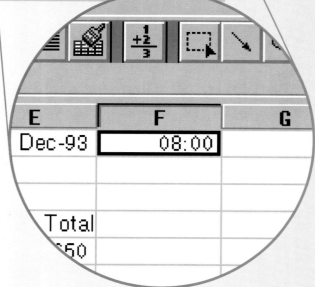

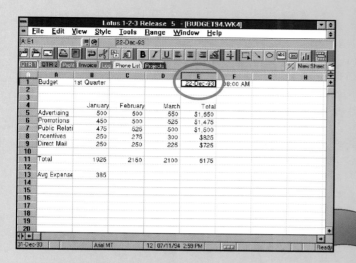

1 Click the **QTR 1** sheet tab to redisplay the first quarter budget sheet. Select cell **E1**. This selects the cell in which you want to format the date.

2 Click the **format selector** on the status bar. This displays a list of number formats. The format selector is the first panel and usually displays Automatic. In the figure, the format selector displays 31-Dec-93.

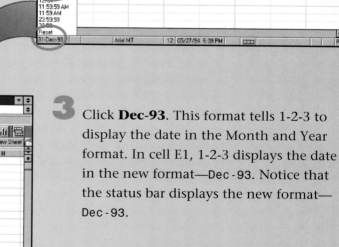

WHY WORRY?

To undo the most recent formatting change, click the **Undo** SmartIcon.

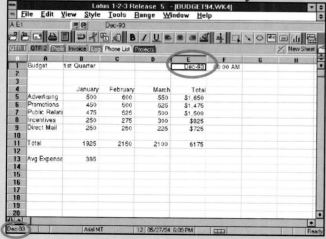

3 Click **Dec-93**. This format tells 1-2-3 to display the date in the Month and Year format. In cell E1, 1-2-3 displays the date in the new format—Dec-93. Notice that the status bar displays the new format—Dec-93.

Task 40: Changing Date and Time Formats

4 Select cell **F1**. This selects cell F1, the time entry you want to format. In the figure, the format selector displays 11:59AM as the current time format.

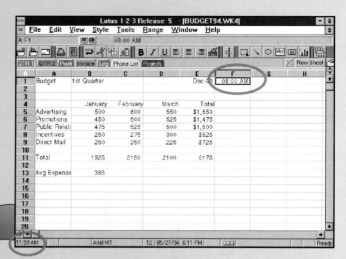

5 Click the **format selector** on the status bar. This displays a list of number formats.

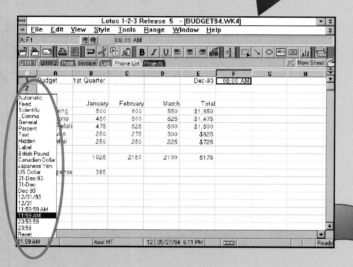

6 Click **23:59**. This format tells 1-2-3 to display the time in the Hour and Minutes format using military time. In cell F1, 1-2-3 displays the time in the new format—08:00. Notice that the status bar displays the new format—23:59.

NOTE

If you see asterisks (*) in the column, the entry is too long to fit. You must increase the column width.

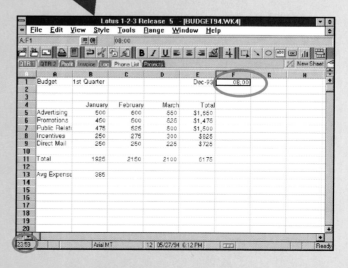

Changing Column Width

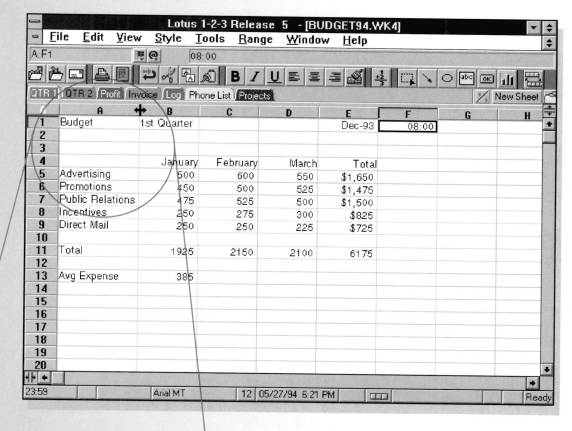

"Why would I do this?"

Asterisks (*) in a cell indicate that the column is not wide enough to display the results of the formula. Often, the formatting (and the selected font) makes the entry longer than the default column width. For example, $3,000 is only six characters, but if you format the number as US Dollar with two decimal places, the number appears as $3,000.00. This number requires nine spaces. You can also adjust the row height to accommodate taller characters if a larger font is selected.

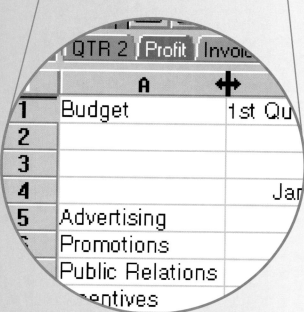

Task 41: Changing Column Width

1 Move the mouse pointer to the line to the right of column letter A. Column A is the column you want to adjust. The mouse pointer changes to a double arrow.

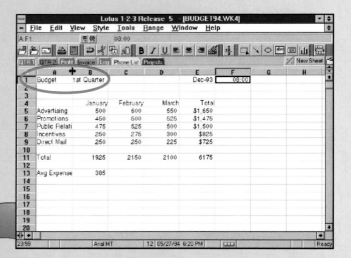

NOTE ▼

You can also double-click the line to the right of the column you want to adjust. Double-clicking the line automatically adjusts the width of the column to accommodate the longest entry in the column.

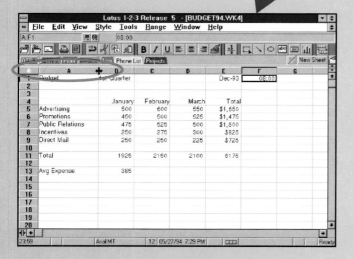

2 Hold down the left mouse button. Drag the mouse to make the column the correct width, then release the mouse button. 1-2-3 widens the column.

NOTE ▼

If some entries still spill into the next column, or if some cells still display asterisks, you must widen the column even more.

WHY WORRY?

To undo the most recent formatting change, click the **Undo** SmartIcon. If you want to reset the column width to the original setting, choose the **Style Column Width** command and click the **Reset to Worksheet Default** option button in the Column Width dialog box.

Changing the Font

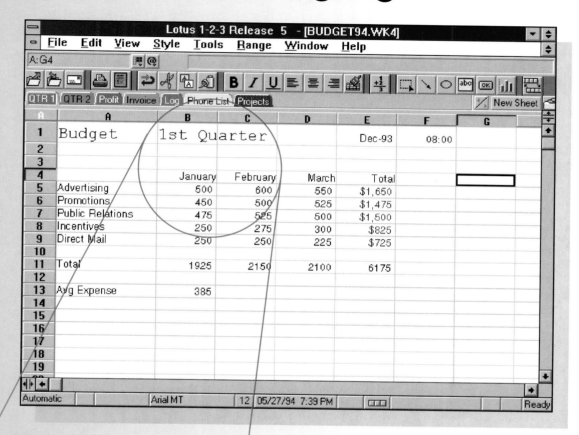

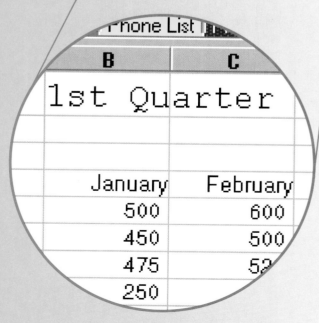

"Why would I do this?"

To emphasize text and numbers in a worksheet, you can change the font, font size, and font color. To enhance the text for a worksheet title, you can change the font to Times New Roman, for example. You can also change the font size to 24-point. There are many font colors in various shades, hues, and patterns you can choose to make your worksheet more attractive.

Task 42: Changing the Font

1 Select cells **A1** and **B1**. This selects the title and subtitle—the text you want to change.

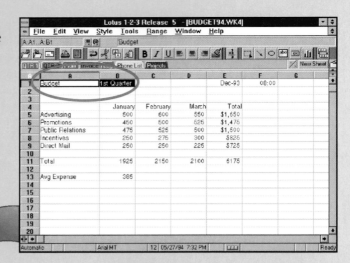

2 Click the **font selector** on the status bar. The font selector is the fourth panel from the left side of the status bar. This displays the list of fonts

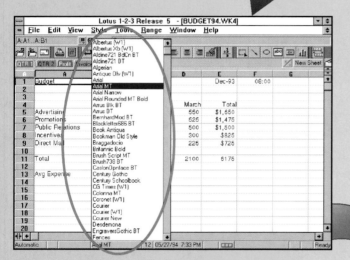

> **NOTE** ▼
>
> The fonts in the list can vary, depending on the type of printer you have and the fonts installed.

3 Click any font in the list, such as Courier New. This changes the font for the text in the selected range. The text appears bigger than it was before because it spills into the adjacent cell. Next, you change the font size to a larger font to emphasize it more.

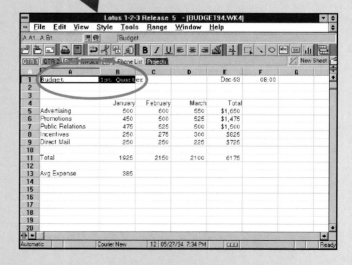

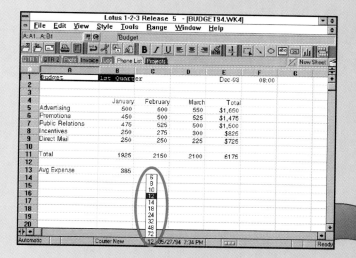

4 With cells A1 and B1 selected, click the **point-size selector** on the status bar. The point-size selector is the fifth panel from the left side of the status bar. This displays the list of font sizes.

> **NOTE** ▼
>
> The font sizes in the list can vary, depending on the type of printer you have and the selected font.

5 Click a larger font size (a higher number), such as 18. This changes the font size for the title and subtitle. Next, bring more attention to the column totals by changing the font color.

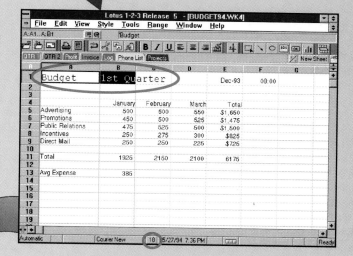

6 Select cells **E5** to **E9**. This selects the range you want to change—E5..E9.

Task 42: Changing the Font

7 Click **Style** in the menu bar. Then, click **Font & Attributes**. 1-2-3 displays the Font & Attributes dialog box.

NOTE ▼

You can also display this dialog box by clicking the **Font & Attributes** SmartIcon on the Formatting palette

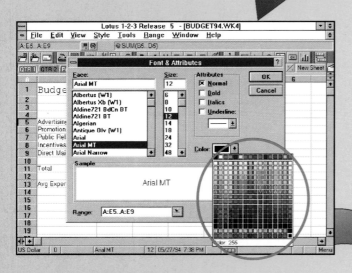

8 Click the down arrow next to **Color**. This displays a palette of colors. The default text color is black.

9 Click any shade of blue in the color palette. We chose color 168. The color number appears at the bottom of the palette. Then click **OK**. You see the color change on-screen. Click any cell to deselect the range.

WHY WORRY?

To undo the font change, font size change, or font color change, immediately click the **Undo** SmartIcon.

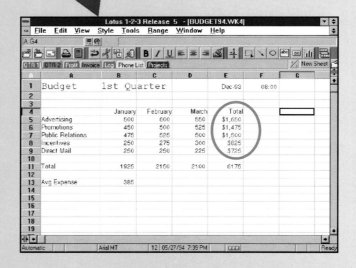

Adding Bold, Italic, and Underline

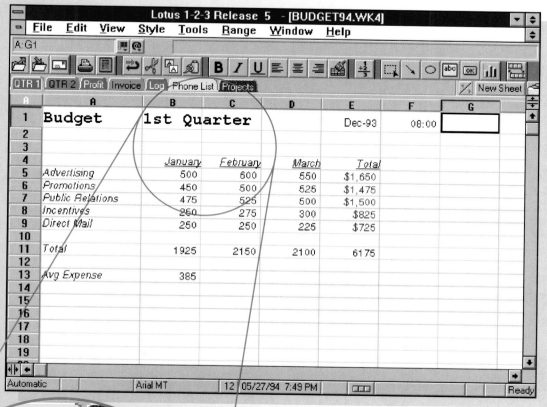

"Why would I do this?"

To emphasize important words and numbers in a worksheet, you can change the font style. You can specify styles such as bold, italic, and underline to highlight significant words and numbers.

Task 43: Adding Bold, Italic, and Underline

1 Select cells **A1** and **B1**. This selects the title and subtitle—the text you want to change.

NOTE ▼

The long subtitle spills into cell C1. You don't have to select cell C1. Only cell B1 contains the text for the long label. 1-2-3 will format the entire label in cell B1.

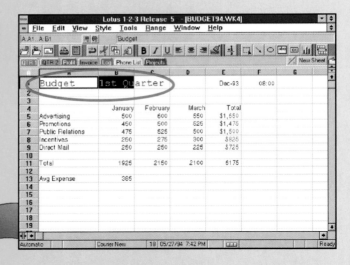

2 Click the **Bold** SmartIcon. Then, click any cell to deselect the range and see the changes. Clicking the Bold SmartIcon applies bold to the selected cells—in this case, A1 and B1.

3 Select cells **B4** to **E4**. Then, select cells **A5** to **A13**. This selects the column headings and row headings—the text you want to change.

NOTE ▼

Hold down the **Ctrl** key while selecting the second range so that you don't deselect the first range.

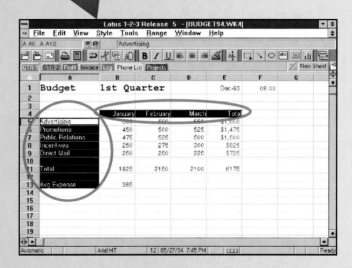

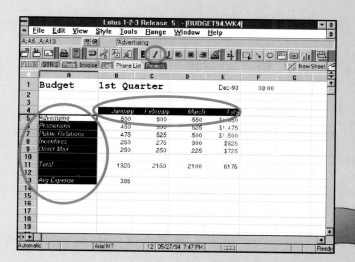

4 Click the **Italic** SmartIcon. Then, click any cell to deselect the range and see the changes. Clicking the Italic SmartIcon italicizes the data in the selected cells—in this case, ranges B4..E4 and A5..A13.

5 Select cells **B4** to **E4**. This selects the column headings—the text you want to change.

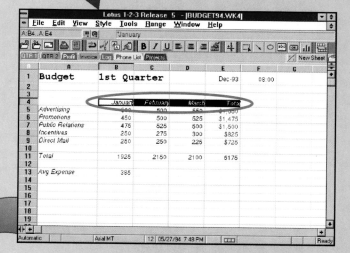

6 Click the **Underline** SmartIcon. Then, click any cell to deselect the range and see the changes. Clicking the Underline SmartIcon underlines the data.

WHY WORRY?

To undo the bold, italic, and underline font styles, select the formatted cell(s) and then click **Bold**, **Italic**, or **Underline** SmartIcon to turn off the style.

TASK 44

Copying Formats

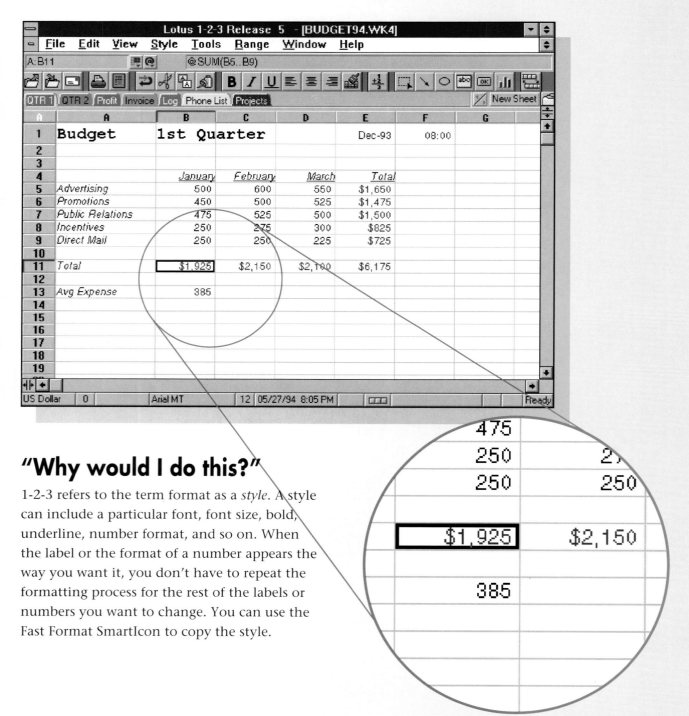

"Why would I do this?"

1-2-3 refers to the term format as a *style*. A style
can include a particular font, font size, bold,
underline, number format, and so on. When
the label or the format of a number appears the
way you want it, you don't have to repeat the
formatting process for the rest of the labels or
numbers you want to change. You can use the
Fast Format SmartIcon to copy the style.

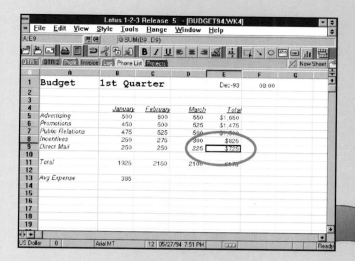

1 Click cell **E9**. This selects the cell that has the formats you want to copy.

WHY WORRY?

To undo the most recent formatting change, click the **Undo** SmartIcon.

2 Click the **Fast Format** SmartIcon. This selects the Style Fast Format command. The prompt `Select cells to format` appears in the title bar.

NOTE ▼

When you move the mouse pointer back into the work area, its shape changes to a paint brush, waiting to "paint" the style in the range(s) you select.

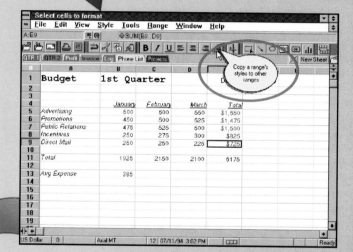

3 Select cells **B11**, **C11**, **D11**, and **E11**. This selects the range B11..E11. The styles from E9 are pasted to the range—in this case, dollar signs, zero decimal places and the blue font color. Press **Esc** to end the pasting.

NOTE ▼

As long as the pointer is still a paint brush, you can select other ranges to paste the same style.

Shading Cells

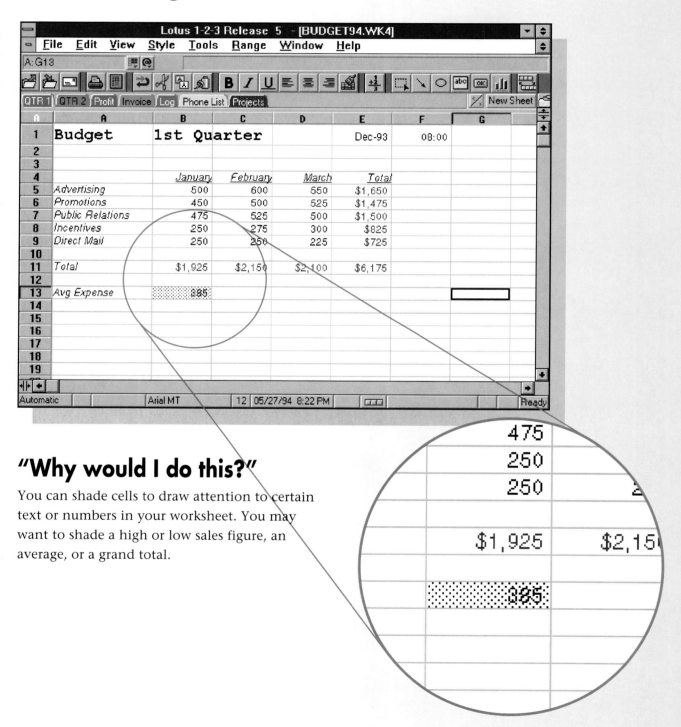

"Why would I do this?"

You can shade cells to draw attention to certain text or numbers in your worksheet. You may want to shade a high or low sales figure, an average, or a grand total.

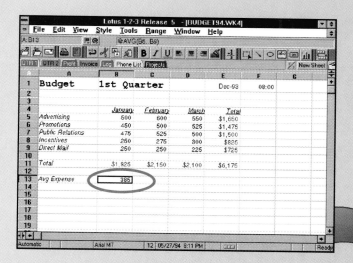

1 Click cell **B13**. This is the cell you want to shade.

2 Click **Style** in the menu bar. Then, click **Lines & Color**. This selects the Style Lines & Color command. 1-2-3 displays the Lines & Color dialog box.

NOTE ▼

You can also display this dialog box by clicking the **Lines & Color** SmartIcon on the Formatting palette.

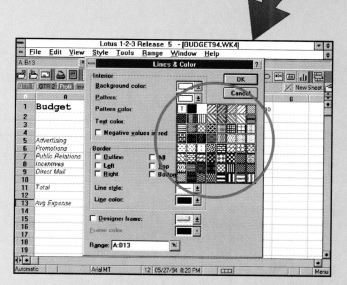

3 Click the **down arrow** next to Pattern. This displays a palette of patterns.

Task 45: Shading Cells

4 In the fourth row of the palette, click the second-to-last pattern. This selects a light dotted pattern. The pattern displays in the Sample area.

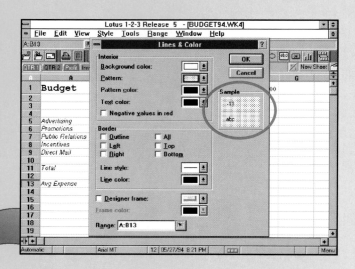

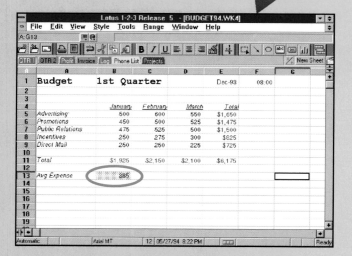

5 Click **OK**. This confirms the change. Then, click any cell to deselect the cell. On-screen, you see the shading in cell B13.

NOTE ▼

Depending on your printer, the shading may print differently than it appears on-screen—or the shading may not print at all.

WHY WORRY?

To remove the shading, immediately click the **Undo** SmartIcon.

Adding Borders

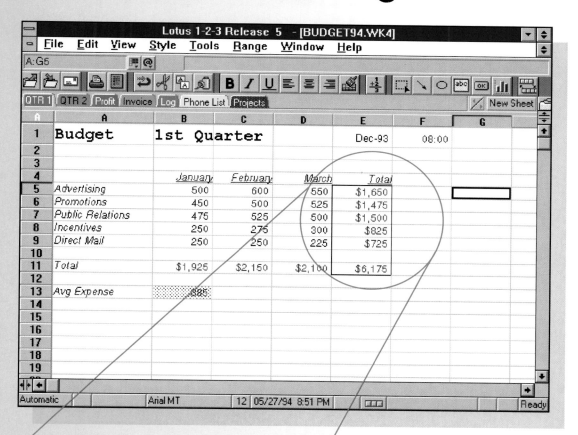

"Why would I do this?"

1-2-3's Style Lines & Color command lets you add boxes around cells and ranges with either a single or double line. For example, you can use a single thick outline border that creates a box to emphasize the title for the worksheet. Or you can use a double underline on the bottom of cells to bring attention to totals.

Task 46: Adding Borders

1 Select cells **E5** to **E11**. This selects the range E5..E11—the range you want to outline.

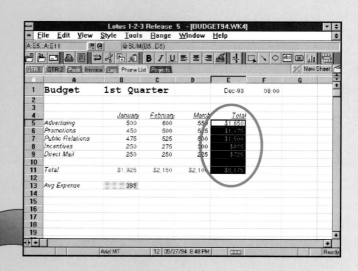

2 Click **Style** in the menu bar, and then click **Lines & Color**. In the Border area, click the **Outline** check box. An X appears in the check box. This selects the Outline option.

WHY WORRY?

To remove the outline, immediately click the **Undo** SmartIcon.

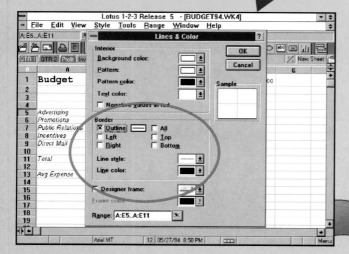

3 Click **OK**. This tells 1-2-3 to outline the edges of the range with a single line. Click any other cell to deselect the range so you can see the outline better.

NOTE

The outline still can be hard to see because the grid lines are displayed on-screen.

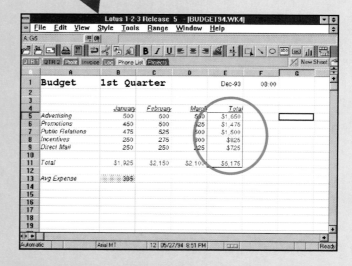

Using Style Templates

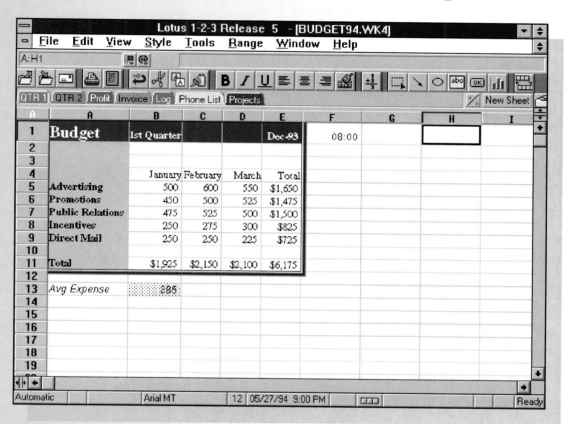

"Why would I do this?"

In 1-2-3, you can apply a set of predefined formats called a *style template* to selected data on the worksheet. Each template contains various alignment, number format, color, and pattern settings. Generally, you apply one format at a time to a selected cell or range of cells. But with a style template, you can apply a collection of formats supplied by 1-2-3 all at once. The style template formats help you create professional-looking worksheets.

Task 47: Using Style Templates

1 Select cells **A1** to **E11**. This selects the range A1..E11—the range you want to format.

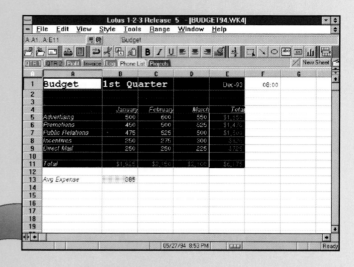

2 Click **Style** in the menu bar. This selects the Style command. 1-2-3 opens the Style menu and displays a list of Style commands.

3 Click **Gallery**. This selects the Gallery command. 1-2-3 displays the Gallery dialog box. A list of templates and a Sample area appear in the box. The Chisel1 template is currently selected.

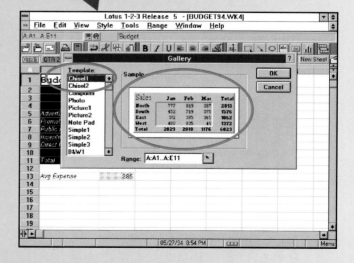

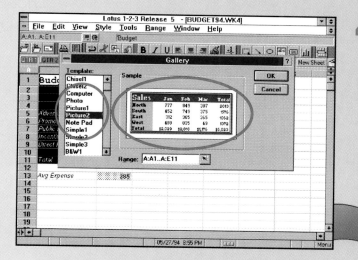

4 Click **Picture2** in the Template list box. This selects the Picture2 template. Notice that a sample of the template appears in the Sample area.

5 Click **OK**. Then, click any cell to deselect the range. This confirms your choice. 1-2-3 changes the worksheet to the new format.

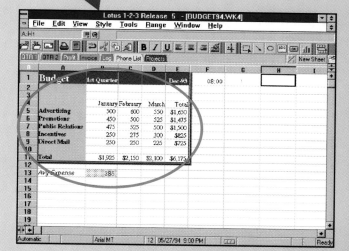

NOTE ▼

This style gallery template has removed the underline and italics from the selected range. These can be added after applying the template. If you plan to use the style gallery, apply it before adding other formatting.

WHY WORRY?

To remove the format, click the SmartIcon. Then repeat the previous steps and choose a different template.

TASK 48

Hiding Grid Lines

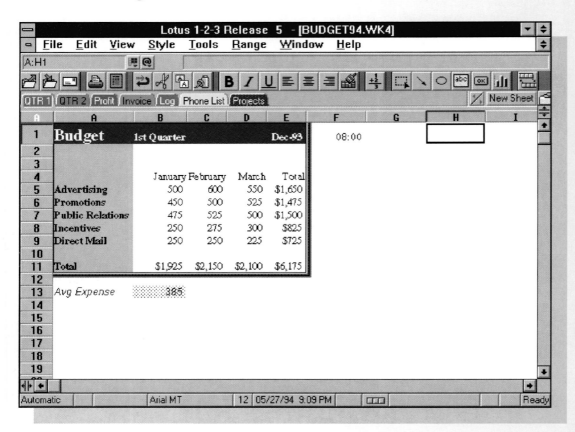

"Why would I do this?"

Another way to make your worksheet look more attractive is to hide the grid lines that separate the cells in the worksheet. Your worksheet seems cleaner on the white background without the grids. You may want to hide grid lines in your worksheets to see how the data looks when printed on white paper.

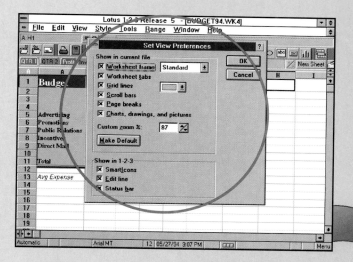

1 Click **View** in the menu bar. Then, click **Set View Preferences**. 1-2-3 displays the Set View Preferences dialog box.

2 Click the check box next to **Grid Lines** in the Show in Current File area. This deselects the Grid Lines option.

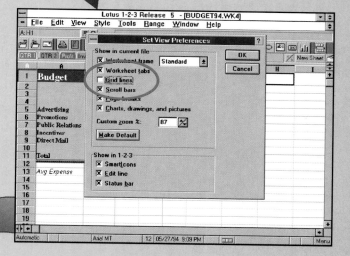

3 Click **OK**. This confirms your choice. As you can see, the grid lines no longer appear in the worksheet. Now click the **Save** SmartIcon to save the file.

WHY WORRY?

If you change your mind and want to turn on the grid lines again, immediately click the **Undo** SmartIcon. Or you can select the **Grid Lines** option in the Set View Preferences dialog box.

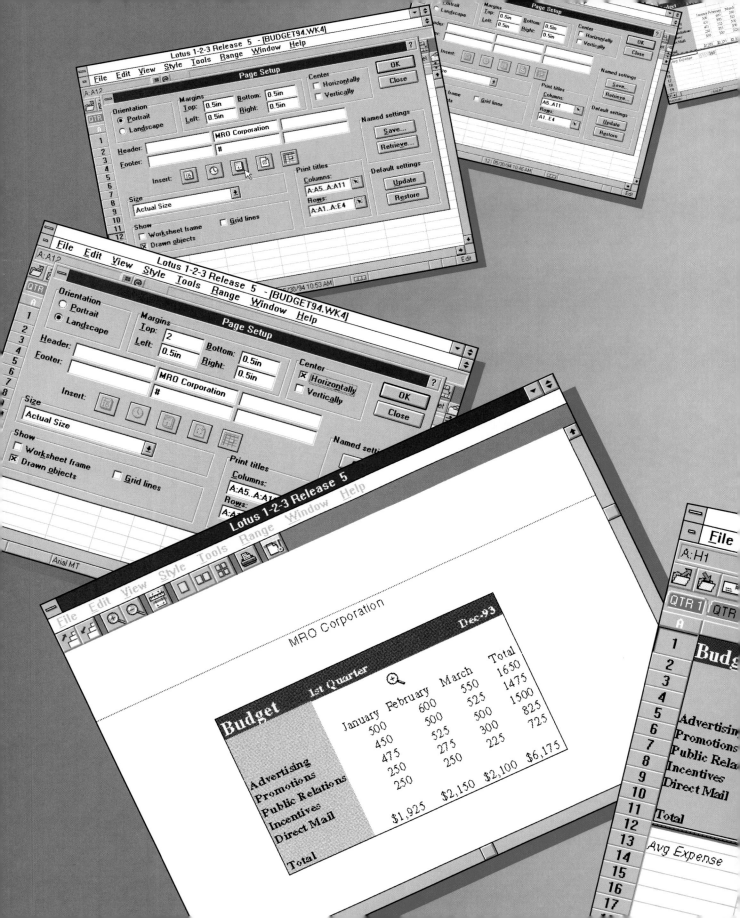

PART VI

Printing the Worksheet

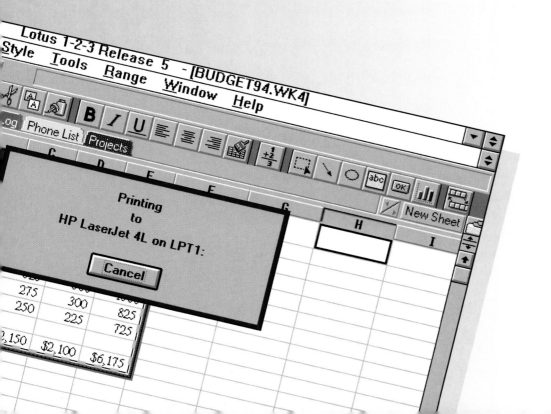

Part VI: Printing the Worksheet

In 1-2-3, you can print your worksheets using a basic printing procedure or you can enhance the printout using several print options. It is fairly simple to print a worksheet in 1-2-3.

First, you set up the format for your printout. You can insert manual page breaks in your worksheet to split the worksheet on two or more pages. Otherwise, 1-2-3 automatically sets the page breaks. Page breaks remain on the worksheet until you remove them. Establishing new page breaks sometimes affects automatic page breaks.

In 1-2-3, you will find most print options in the Page Setup dialog box. The Page Setup dialog box contains options for specifying the layout for a printed page and lets you create headers and footers.

For large worksheets, you may want to print column headings at the top with the Print Titles Columns option. You can print row headings at the left side of each page with the Print Titles Rows option.

With 1-2-3's Print Preview feature, you can review the appearance of the printed worksheet before you produce the final output. The first page of the worksheet appears as a reduced image in the Print Preview screen. However, you can zoom in on the Print Preview to magnify the view or zoom out to reduce the view to a smaller image. You can also change the margins and page setup, and start printing from the Preview window.

The first time you use your printer with 1-2-3, it is a good idea to check the Setup options. 1-2-3 can use the options and capabilities that are available with each printer. Often, you will need to provide more details about your printer so that 1-2-3 knows the capabilities available. If you want to specify details about your printer, choose the File Printer Setup command. Then you can confirm that you installed the right printer and connected it correctly, or you can switch to a different printer.

The options in the Page Setup dialog box control print enhancements such as orientation, margins, and the size of the printout. The default print orientation is Portrait, which means that the worksheet prints vertically on the paper. You can choose Landscape to print the worksheet sideways (or horizontally) on the paper. If the worksheet is too wide, you can try decreasing the widths of some columns if possible.

If the worksheet is still too large to print on one page, you can change the top, bottom, left, and right margins. You also may consider reducing the printout using the Size option in the Page Setup dialog box. Some printers will let you reduce or enlarge the printout as it prints. The Size options include Actual Size, Fit All to Page, Fit Columns to Page, Fit Rows to Page, and Manually Scale. See your Lotus 1-2-3 documentation for complete information.

1-2-3 lets you add headers and footers to print information at the top and bottom of every page of the printout. You can include any text plus special commands to control the appearance of the header or footer.

It is a good idea to experiment with all the print options until you get the results you want. It is also recommended that you save your worksheets before printing—just in case a printer error or other problem occurs. You won't lose any work if you saved the worksheet. If you already set up your print options and you're back to the worksheet, you can just click the Print SmartIcon to print your worksheet quickly.

The Print dialog box lets you print some or all the sheets within a worksheet, a selected range, a range of pages, and multiple copies of the printout.

This part introduces you to the basics of printing the worksheet. With some experimentation and practice, you will be able to create some very interesting print results.

Inserting and Removing Page Breaks

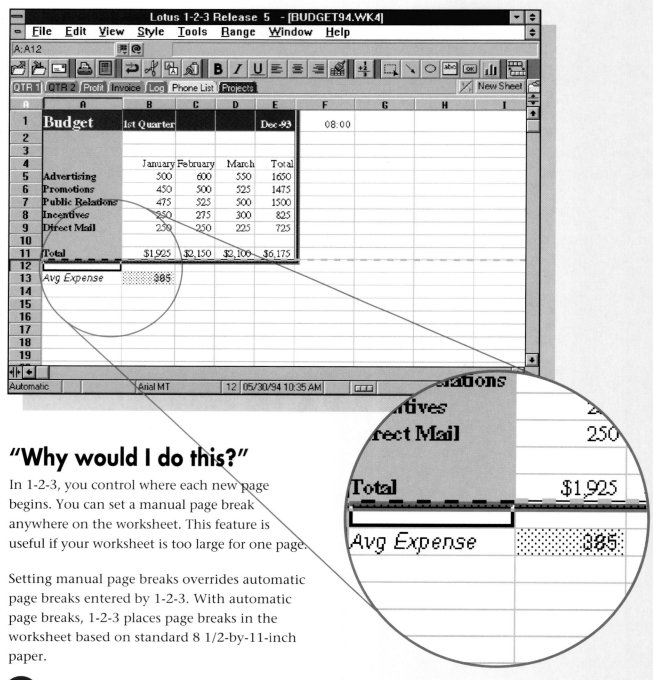

"Why would I do this?"

In 1-2-3, you control where each new page begins. You can set a manual page break anywhere on the worksheet. This feature is useful if your worksheet is too large for one page.

Setting manual page breaks overrides automatic page breaks entered by 1-2-3. With automatic page breaks, 1-2-3 places page breaks in the worksheet based on standard 8 1/2-by-11-inch paper.

Task 49: Inserting and Removing Page Breaks

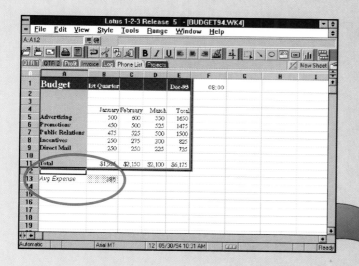

1 Click cell **A12**. A12 is the cell below where you want to insert a page break. 1-2-3 will print everything above row 12 on one page and everything below row 12 on the next page.

2 Click **Style** in the menu bar. Then, click **Page Break**. This selects the Style Page Break command. 1-2-3 opens the Page Break dialog box.

NOTE ▼

If you click a cell that is not in the far left column of the worksheet and then select the **Options Set Page Break** command, 1-2-3 inserts manual page breaks above and to the left of the selected cell.

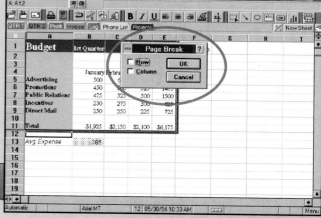

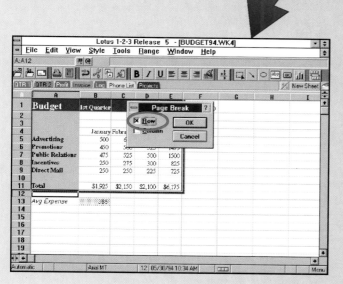

3 Click the check box next to **Row**. This selects the Row option, which tells 1-2-3 to insert a horizontal page break.

4 Click **OK**. This confirms your choice. The manual horizontal page break appears above the active cell.

> **NOTE** ▼
>
> On-screen, manual page breaks have longer, thicker dashed lines than automatic page breaks. These page breaks may be hard to see when grid lines also appear on-screen.

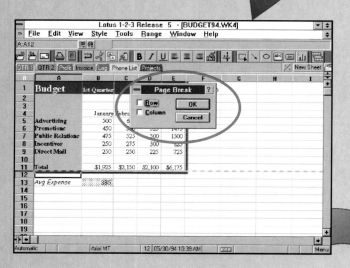

5 With cell A12 selected, click **Style** in the menu bar. Then, click **Page Break**. 1-2-3 opens the Page Break dialog box. Click the check box next to **Row**. This removes the X in the Row check box, deselecting the Row option.

6 Click **OK**. The manual horizontal page break disappears above the active cell.

> **NOTE** ▼
>
> If you insert the page break in the wrong place, just click the **Undo** SmartIcon. Or select the cell immediately below or to the right of the page break line(s). Then, delete the page break with the **Style Page Break** command.

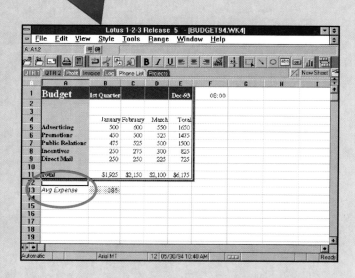

Printing Column and Row Headings

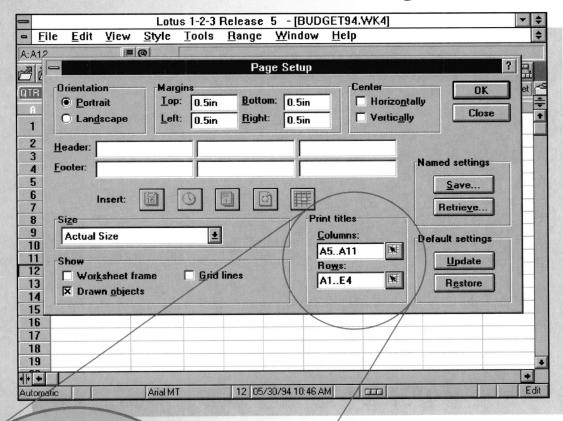

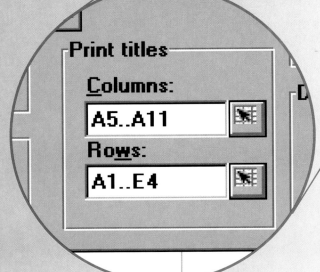

"Why would I do this?"

1-2-3 lets you select labels and titles that are located on the left side and top edge of your worksheet and print them on every page of the printout. This option is useful when a worksheet is too wide to print on a single page. Unless you use the Print Titles Columns and Print Titles Rows options, the extra columns will print on subsequent pages without any descriptive information.

Task 50: Printing Column and Row Headings

1 Click **File** in the menu bar. Then, click **Page Setup**. This selects the File Page Setup command. 1-2-3 displays the Page Setup dialog box.

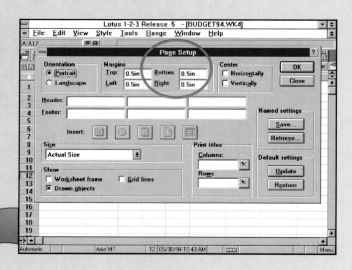

2 Click in the **Columns** text box. The insertion point appears in the box. Then, type A5..A11. This specifies the range A5..A11—the range you want to repeat at the left side of every page.

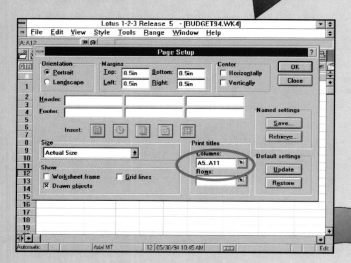

NOTE ▼

On-screen, you cannot see any changes after you click OK. When you print a worksheet that contains multiple pages, however, you will see the title, column and row headings on every page.

3 Click in the **Rows** text box or press the **Tab** key. Then, type A1..E4. This specifies the range you want to repeat at the top of every page. Click **OK**.

WHY WORRY?

To remove the columns and rows you want to repeat, click the **Undo** SmartIcon. Or you can delete the cell coordinates in the Print Titles Columns and Print Titles Rows text boxes.

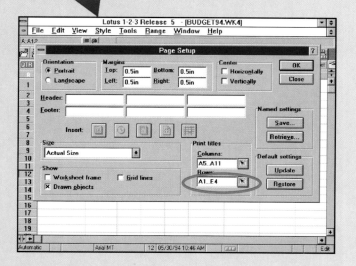

Adding Headers and Footers

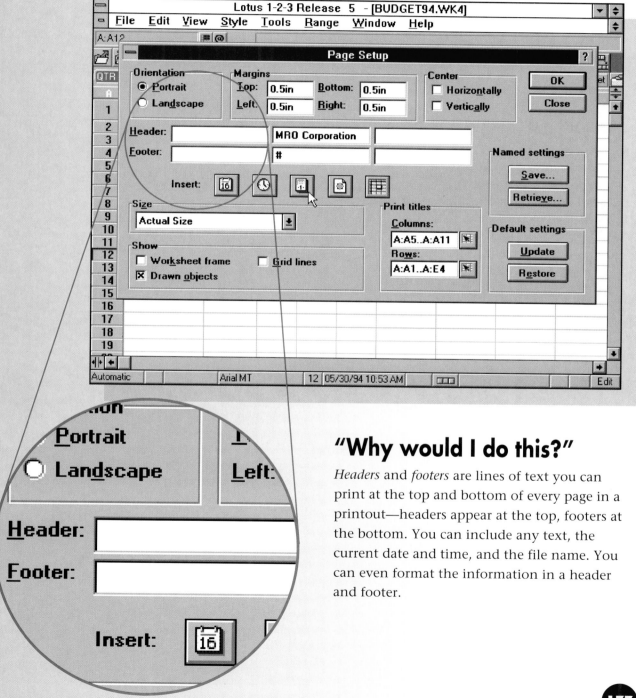

"Why would I do this?"

Headers and *footers* are lines of text you can print at the top and bottom of every page in a printout—headers appear at the top, footers at the bottom. You can include any text, the current date and time, and the file name. You can even format the information in a header and footer.

Task 51: Adding Headers and Footers

1 Click **File** in the menu bar. Then, click **Page Setup**. This selects the File Page Setup command. 1-2-3 opens the Page Setup dialog box.

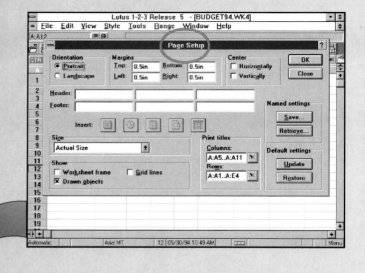

> **NOTE** ▼
>
> You can format headers left, center, and right. You can also include codes in the header or footer. Refer to your Lotus 1-2-3 documentation for a complete list of formatting options and codes.

2 Click in the center **Header** text box. The insertion point appears in the center position. Type **MRO Corporation**.

3 Click in the center **Footer** text box. The insertion point appears in the center box. Click the **Page Number** icon next to the Insert options (the icon has a page with the number -1- at the bottom). This inserts a code (#) that tells 1-2-3 to insert the page number. When you print the document, the code will be replaced by the appropriate page number. Click **OK**.

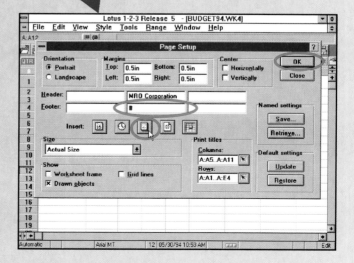

Setting Margins, Orientation, and Page Centering

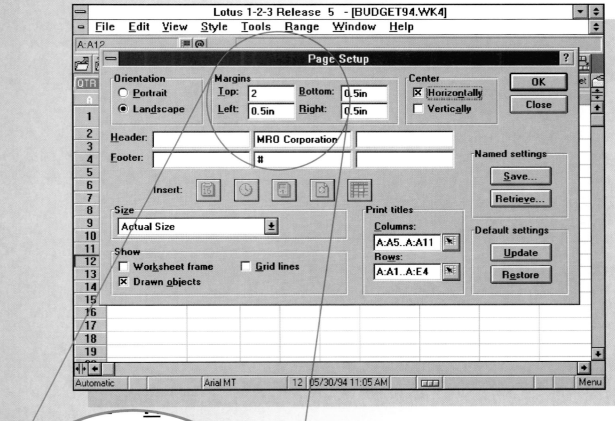

"Why would I do this?"

If you have a large worksheet that you want to fit on one page or as few pages as possible, you may want to change the top, bottom, left, and right margins. The default setting for each margin is 0.5". If you have a very large worksheet, you may want to print the worksheet in landscape orientation. You can also choose to center the print selection vertically and/or horizontally on the page.

Task 52: Setting Margins, Orientation, and Page Centering

1 Click **File** in the menu bar. Then, click **Page Setup**. This selects the File Page Setup command. 1-2-3 opens the Page Setup dialog box.

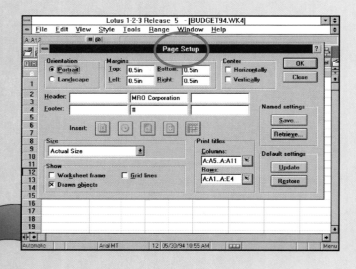

2 Click in the **Top** text box in the Margins area. This selects the Top margin setting—the setting you want to change. Type **2**. This sets the new top margin to 2 inches. 1-2-3 will automatically insert in (for inches) after the 2.

> **NOTE** ▼
>
> You also can change the Bottom, Left, and Right margin settings in the Margins dialog box.

3 Click **Landscape** in the Orientation area. This selects the Landscape option button and specifies Landscape orientation.

> **NOTE** ▼
>
> You cannot see the new orientation on-screen. To do so, you must preview the worksheet.

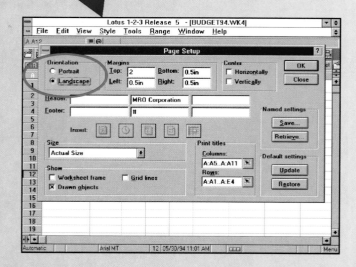

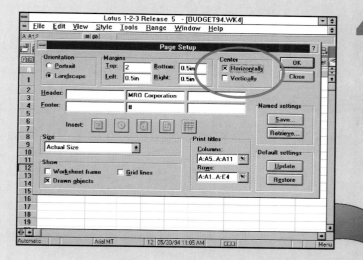

4 Click **Horizontally** in the Center area. This will center the selection horizontally on the printed page.

NOTE ▼

To center the page vertically, click **Vertically**. You can click both **Horizontally** and **Vertically** to center both directions.

5 Click **OK**. These Page Setup changes are not visible in the worksheet. See the next task on previewing the print job to see the effects of the settings.

WHY WORRY?

Click the **Undo** SmartIcon immediately to undo these page setup changes—even before you preview the worksheet. Or follow this same procedure to modify the settings again.

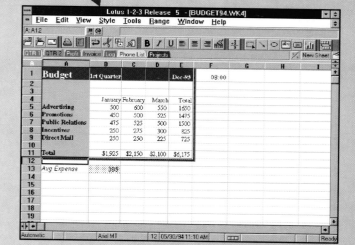

Previewing the Print Job

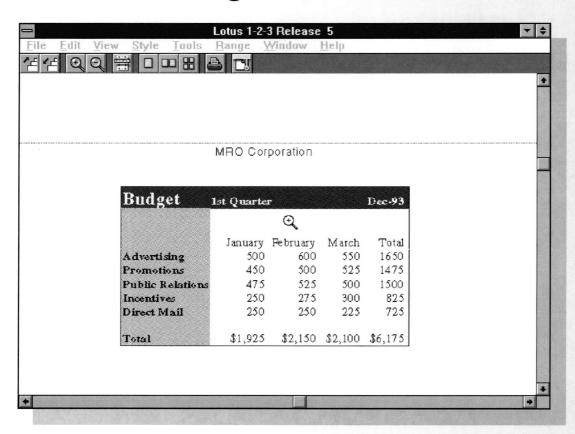

"Why would I do this?"

The Print Preview command lets you see worksheet pages on-screen as they will appear printed on paper, including page numbers, headers, footers, fonts, fonts sizes and styles, orientation, and margins. Previewing your worksheet is a great way to catch formatting errors, such as incorrect margins, overlapped data, boldfaced data, and other text enhancements. You save costly printer paper and time by first previewing your worksheet.

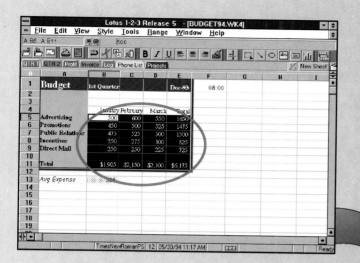

1 Select cells **B5** to **E11**. This selects the range you want to print—in this case, B5..E11.

> **NOTE** ▼
>
> Be sure that you don't select the data you already included in the column and row print titles. Otherwise, 1-2-3 will print the column and row titles twice.

2 Click the **Print Preview** SmartIcon (the icon is represented by a piece of paper with marks that look like text). Clicking the Print Preview SmartIcon selects the Print Preview command. 1-2-3 opens the Print Preview dialog box.

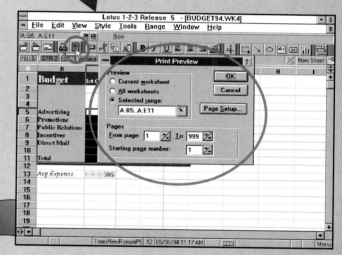

3 Click **OK**. You see a preview of how your worksheet will look when you print it. Click the preview. The mouse pointer is shaped like a magnifying glass with a plus sign (+) in it. This is the Zoom In pointer. The preview enlarges.

> **NOTE** ▼
>
> You can click again to zoom closer, and then click once more to return to the full page preview. To exit the preview, click the **Close** SmartIcon (which looks like a window shade) or press **Esc**.

TASK 54

Printing the Worksheet

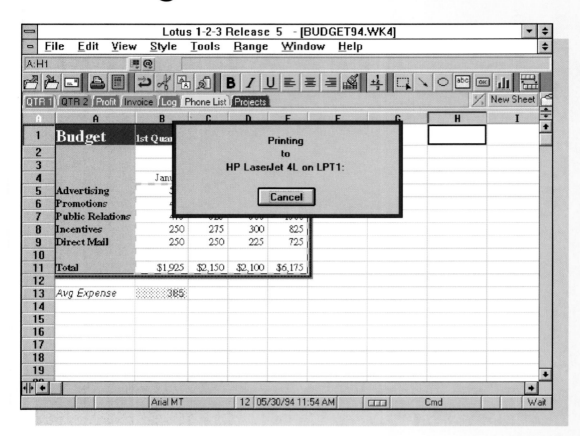

"Why would I do this?"

1-2-3 offers many print options and features. You can print only the current worksheet, all worksheets, a selected range, a range of pages, and multiple copies of your worksheet. For complete information, see your Lotus 1-2-3 documentation.

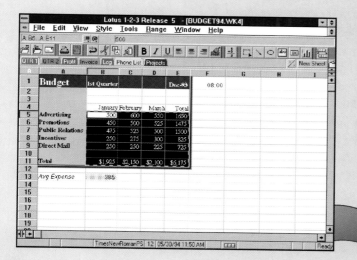

1 Select cells **B5** to **E11**. This selects the range you want to print. The range excludes row and column headings that are already set up to print on each page.

NOTE ▼

If you used Print Preview, the print range is already bordered by gray dashed lines. You do not need to select it again.

2 Click **File** in the menu bar. Then, click **Print**. This selects the File Print command. 1-2-3 displays the Print dialog box. You see the name of your printer at the top of the dialog box.

NOTE ▼

You also can click the **Print** SmartIcon to select the File Print command.

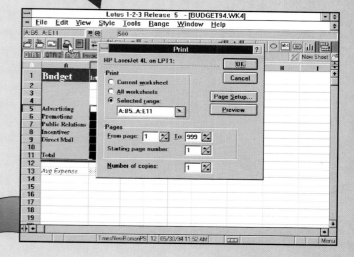

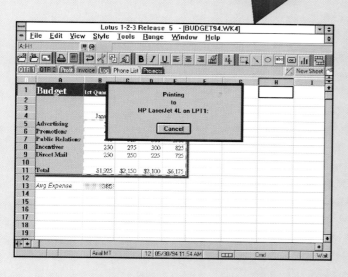

3 Click **OK**. The gray border on the work-sheet area indicates the print range—the area of the worksheet that will be printed.

NOTE ▼

If no printer is installed, refer to the 1-2-3 manual.

WHY WORRY?

To stop the print job, click **Cancel** in the on-screen dialog box.

Part VII: Working with Charts and Maps

After you create your worksheets, you use the information in one type of presentation or another. Simply print the worksheet if you only need numerical detail, or transform the data in the worksheet into a chart. Charts are great for visually representing relationships between numerical values while enhancing a presentation at the same time.

In 1-2-3, you can create a chart directly on the worksheet. An *embedded chart* is a graphic object—a pictorial representation of the data—that appears on the worksheet, along with your worksheet data. You can print any or all of the parts of a worksheet including its data, graphics, and charts. Save a chart with the File Save command as you would any file.

1-2-3 displays the Chart SmartIcons when you select a chart in a worksheet. Use the Chart SmartIcons to change the chart type and to add grid lines and a legend. You also can use the Text SmartIcon to add text labels to your charts.

You should familiarize yourself with the elements of a chart before you create one. The *data series* can be bars, pie slices, lines, or other elements that represent plotted values in a chart. For example, a chart may show a set of bars that have the same pattern; these bars reflect a series of values for the same item—for example, monthly sales figures.

The *chart text* is all of the descriptive labels on the chart. Text is useful for explaining various elements on the chart. You can position the labels (text) wherever you want them to appear on the chart.

The *y-axis* is the vertical axis. It represents the values of the bars, lines, or plot points. 1-2-3 automatically assigns values to this axis when you create a chart, but you can override the default settings and set the minimum and maximum values. You can also add a text label to the y-axis to describe what the values represent.

The *x-axis* is the horizontal axis. This axis contains the data ranges and the X data range in the chart. If your chart contains more than one category, 1-2-3 displays labels that identify each category.

The *plot area* consists of the actual bars, lines, or other elements that represent the data series. Everything outside the plot area helps explain what is inside the plot area. You can format the plot area by changing the patterns and colors of the data ranges.

A *legend* contains the series labels in the chart data. By default, the legend appears to the right of the chart data. However, you can move the legend anywhere you want on the chart. 1-2-3 matches the labels with the data ranges and provides a "key" to the chart.

Grid lines are dotted lines you add to a chart so you can read the plotted data more easily. You can create three types of grid lines: horizontal, vertical, and a combination of both. After you add the grid lines, you can change their colors and patterns.

1-2-3 offers many chart types for presenting your data. You can change the chart type at any time. The chart types you can choose from include: line, area, bar, pie, XY (scatter), HLCO (High-Low-Close-Open for tracking stock), mixed (bar and line), radar, 3-D line, 3-D area, 3-D bar, and 3-D pie.

Geographic data can be represented on a map. This is more visually appealing than using the chart types. Set up a worksheet using data correlated with state or country codes, and then use the map feature to link the data to a map of the geographic region.

You may try experimenting with chart features to create the most attractive and meaningful chart you can. You will see that charting is really very simple to do. By the end of this section, you will be able to create a chart that is perfect for any presentation.

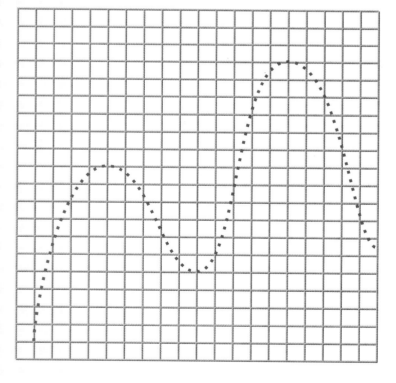

Creating a Chart

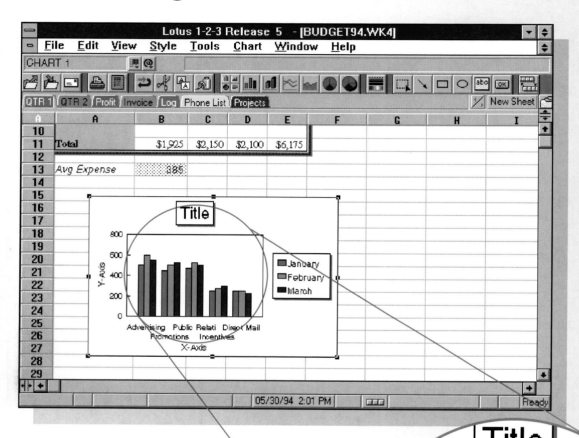

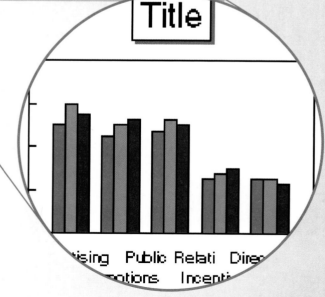

"Why would I do this?"

You can use charts to represent data visually. The easiest way to create a chart in 1-2-3 is to use the Tools Chart command. The default chart type is the bar chart. 1-2-3 plots the data and creates the chart where you specify on the worksheet. Even if you are a novice at creating charts, you will find that transforming the worksheet data into a chart is a breeze.

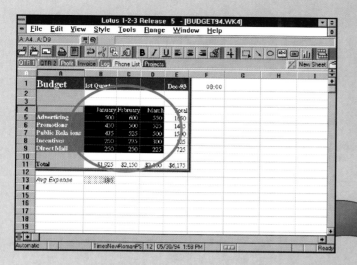

1 Select cells **A4** to **D9**. This selects the range A4..D9—the range you want to chart.

NOTE ▼

Remember, you must first select data before you can create a chart. Don't include the totals in the range.

2 Click **Tools** in the menu bar. Then, click **Chart**. The mouse pointer changes to a cross-hair pointer with a dashed line and a tiny bar chart. 1-2-3 displays the following prompt in the title bar: `Click and drag where you want to display the chart.`

NOTE ▼

The cross-hair chart pointer lets you specify where you want to place the chart on the worksheet.

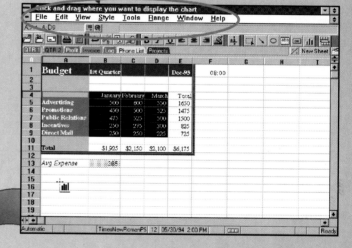

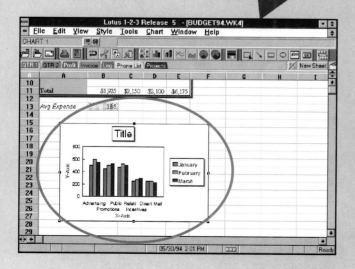

3 Click cell **A15**. This tells 1-2-3 where to place the top left corner of the chart. Click the **Save** SmartIcon to save the worksheet with the chart.

NOTE ▼

The chart is selected—small black squares called *handles* appear around the edges, and 1-2-3 displays Chart SmartIcons. You can change the chart size, location, and type when the chart is selected.

Printing a Chart

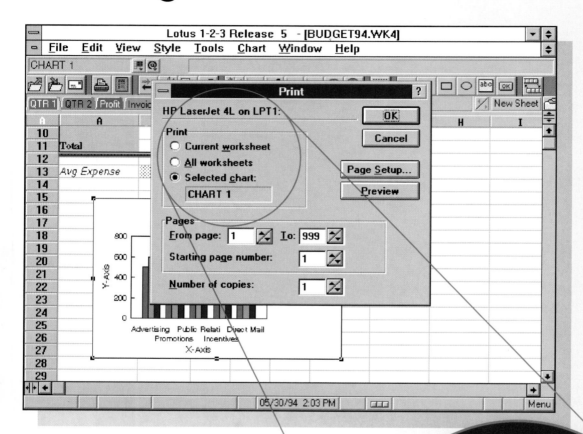

"Why would I do this?"

You can print the embedded chart with its
worksheet as you would any worksheet. You
may want to print the chart and worksheet
together for a presentation. That way, you can
easily see trends in a series of values.

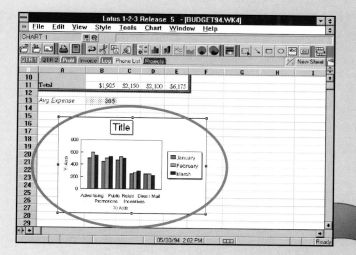

1 Click the chart border, if necessary. This selects the chart. Handles appear along the edges of the chart.

NOTE ▼

Be careful not to select individual items in the chart—the whole chart should be selected.

2 Click the **Print** SmartIcon. Clicking the Print SmartIcon displays the Print dialog box. Notice that CHART1 is selected as the item to print. Click **OK** to confirm that you want to print. 1-2-3 prints the chart.

NOTE ▼

Select the **Current worksheet** option if you want to print both the data and the chart.

WHY WORRY?

During a print job, 1-2-3 displays a dialog box on-screen. To stop the print job, click **Cancel**.

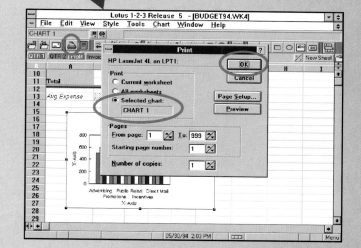

Moving and Resizing a Chart

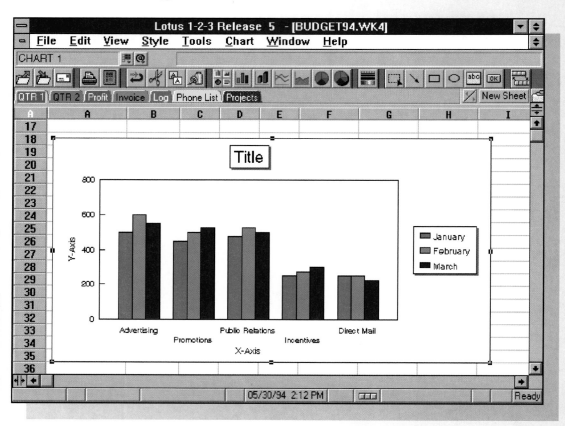

"Why would I do this?"

When you created the chart, you may have placed it in the wrong location. Maybe the chart is too close or too far away from the worksheet data. If you want the chart in a different location on the worksheet, you can move the chart. 1-2-3 creates the chart in the default size. If you want to shrink the chart or make it taller, you can resize the chart after it's on the worksheet.

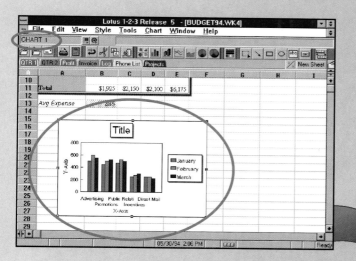

1 Click the chart border to select the chart. Handles appear on the outside of the entire chart when the entire chart is selected, and CHART1 appears in the selection indicator box.

NOTE ▼

Be careful not to select individual items in the chart—the whole chart should be selected.

2 Drag the chart to the right, moving the right edge of the chart into column I. Dragging moves the chart to another location in the worksheet.

NOTE ▼

Notice that the mouse pointer changes its shape to a hand when you are dragging the chart. When the mouse pointer is inside the chart, the pointer changes to an arrow and a small black square.

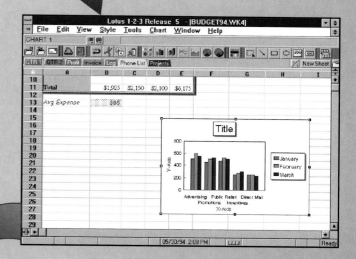

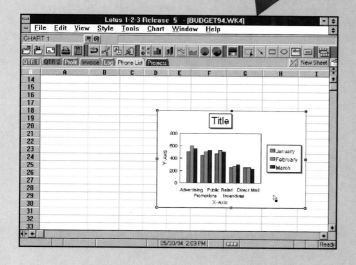

3 Align the chart with the bottom edge of row 30. This moves the chart down. After you place the chart where you want it, you can use the selection handles to change the chart's size and shape.

Task 57: Moving and Resizing a Chart

4 Move the mouse pointer to the left middle handle. When the cursor becomes a four-headed arrow, drag the chart to the left, aligning the chart with the left edge of column A. This makes the chart wider.

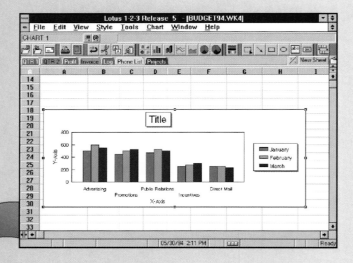

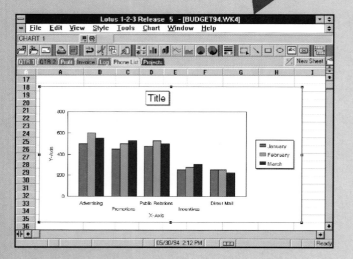

5 Move the mouse pointer to the bottom middle handle. When the cursor changes to a four-headed arrow, drag the chart down to the bottom edge of row 35. This makes the chart taller.

WHY WORRY?

If you don't like the size and shape of the chart, drag the handles in the direction you want until you get the desired results.

Changing the Chart Type

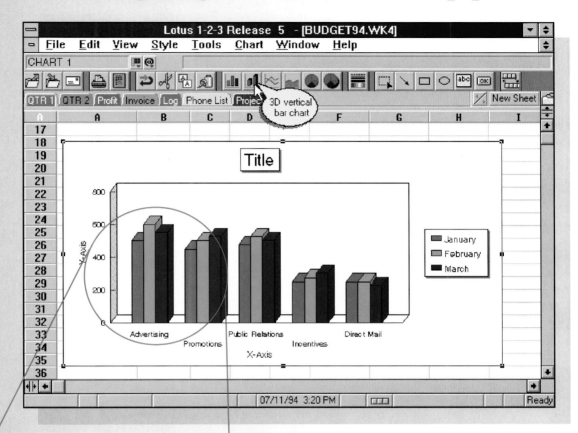

"Why would I do this?"

You can change an existing chart into a different chart at any time. You will find that certain chart types are best for certain situations. It may be more dramatic, appropriate, or meaningful to display the data in a different type of chart. For example, you can usually spot trends more easily with a line chart, while a pie chart is best for showing parts of a whole. A line chart shows trends over time.

Task 58: Changing the Chart Type

1 Click the chart border, if necessary. This selects the chart. Handles appear along the edges of the chart, and CHART1 appears in the selection indicator box.

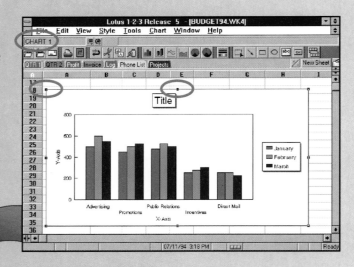

2 Click the **Vertical Line Chart** SmartIcon. The Vertical Line Chart SmartIcon contains two wavy horizontal lines. This selects the vertical line chart type. 1-2-3 changes the chart to reflect your choice. Notice that the lines represent the expenses by month. It is easier to depict trends in the bar chart than in the line chart.

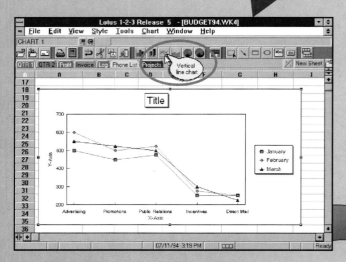

3 Click the **3D Vertical Bar Chart** SmartIcon. The 3D Vertical Bar Chart SmartIcon contains two three-dimensional bars. This selects the 3D vertical bar chart type. 1-2-3 changes the chart to the bar format, showing 3D vertical bars. This looks like a good representation for your data; however, switch to the 3D pie chart.

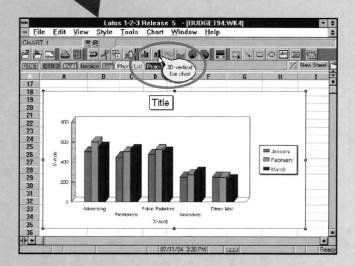

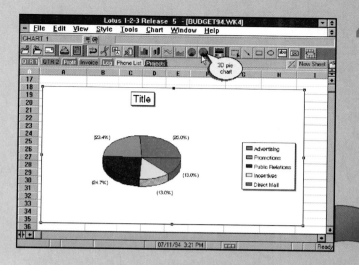

4 Click the 3D Pie Chart SmartIcon, which shows a circle with various colors of sectors. This selects the 3D pie chart type. 1-2-3 changes the chart to a pie chart, showing "pieces" of the pie which represent the percentage of each expense over the total January expense.

NOTE ▼

The pie chart is not a good representation for the data selected in this worksheet, since only the January values will be shown.

5 Click the **Vertical Area Chart** SmartIcon, which contains a wavy horizontal line, and the filled-in area below the line. This selects the vertical area chart type. 1-2-3 changes the chart to the vertical area chart format, showing lines with the areas filled in with color. The maximum number on the vertical axis scale changed from 800 to 2000. The vertical area chart doesn't depict the data as well as the vertical bar chart. Switch back to the vertical bar chart type.

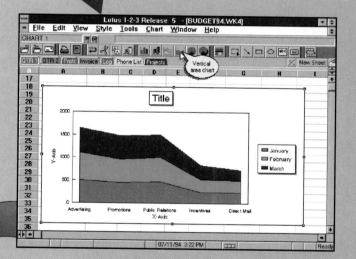

6 Click the **Vertical Bar Chart** SmartIcon. The Vertical Bar Chart SmartIcon contains three vertical bars. This selects the vertical bar chart type.

WHY WORRY?

If the chart type you choose is not what you want, just click another chart type SmartIcon. Or you can select the **Chart Type** command and choose a different chart type in the Type dialog box.

Changing the Title

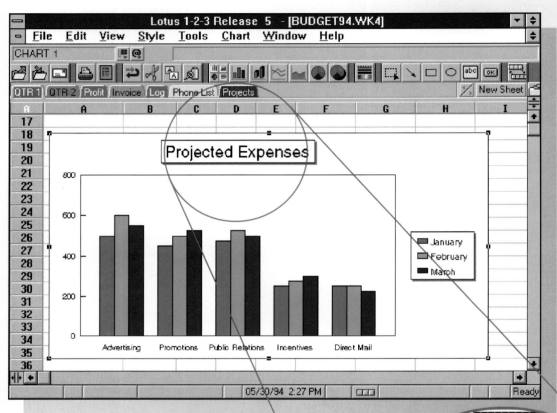

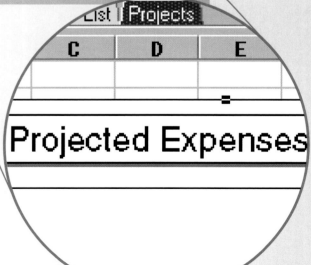

"Why would I do this?"

1-2-3 gives you a generic title when you create a chart. The name Title appears in a shadow box at the top center of the chart. You can change this generic title to the title you want. You can even add a subtitle, too. You may want to add a subtitle to the chart to clearly define what the chart represents.

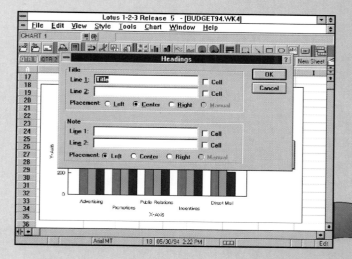

1 Double-click the title at the top of the chart. This displays the Headings dialog box.

2 Double-click in the Line 1 text box. Then, type **Projected Expenses**. This enters the text for the title.

> **NOTE** ▼
>
> You can make the title and subtitle appear on the left, center, or right side at the top of the chart. You can also use the mouse to move a title anywhere you want on the chart.

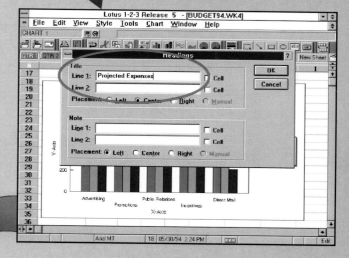

3 Click **OK**. This confirms the new title and closes the dialog box. You see the new title on-screen.

4 Click the label X-Axis. The x-axis title is located below the x-axis labels. This selects the x-axis title. Handles appear along the edges of the title.

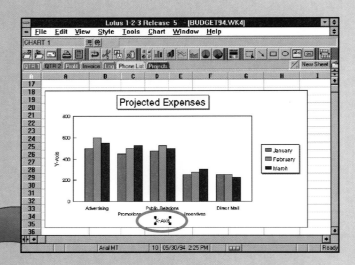

5 Press **Del**. This deletes the x-axis title. 1-2-3 removes the x-axis title at the bottom of the chart.

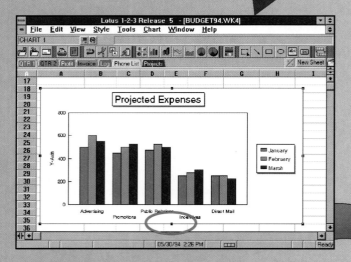

6 Click the label **Y-Axis**. The y-axis title is located on the left side of the y-axis scale. This selects the y-axis title. Handles appear along the edges of the title. Press **Del**. This deletes the y-axis title. 1-2-3 removes the y-axis title on the left side of the chart.

WHY WORRY?

To undo the change, immediately click the **Undo** SmartIcon.

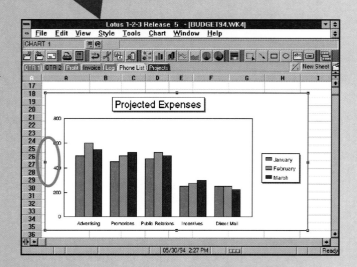

Adding a Legend

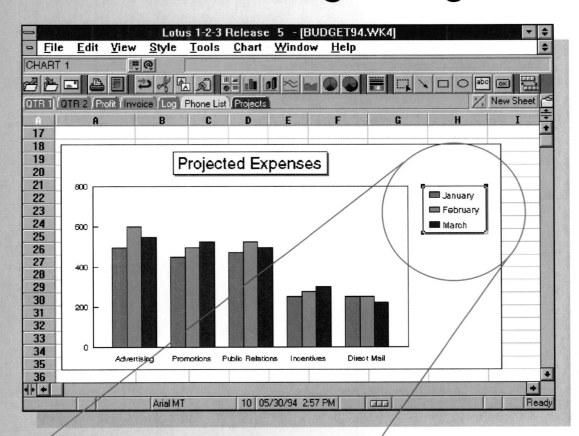

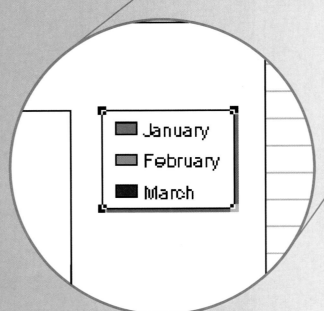

"Why would I do this?"

A chart legend describes the data series and data points; it provides a "key" to the chart. After you add a legend to your chart, you can change the placement of the legend. You may want to add a legend to your chart to clearly describe the data series in the chart's columns. In our chart, the legend already appears on the right side. When you create a chart, adding a legend is the default legend setting.

Task 60: Adding a Legend

1 Click the legend. This selects the legend. A border with handles (small black squares) surrounds the legend.

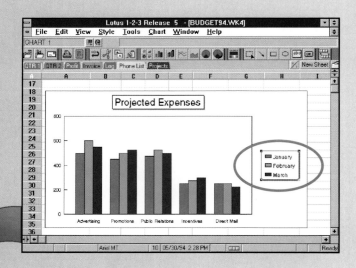

2 Move the mouse pointer to the legend border and drag the legend to the upper right corner of the plot area, aligning it with the top right edge of the plot area (as shown in the figure). This moves the legend to the new location.

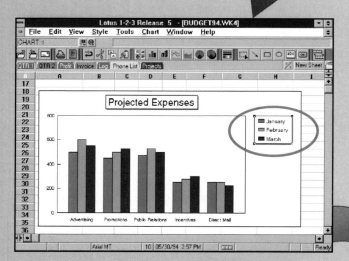

NOTE ▼

The legend series names **January**, **February**, and **March**, are assigned automatically from the worksheet range selected. You can change these names if desired.

3 Double-click the legend. The Legend dialog box is displayed. To change the name of a legend series, click the series name, deselect the **Cell** check box, and type a new series name in the **Legend Entry** text box. Click **OK** to return to the chart.

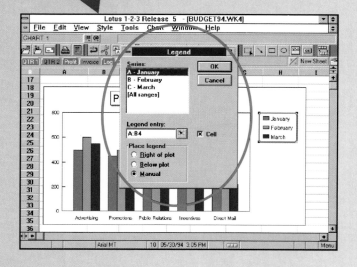

WHY WORRY?

To remove the legend, click the legend to select it, and then press **Del**.

Adding Grid Lines

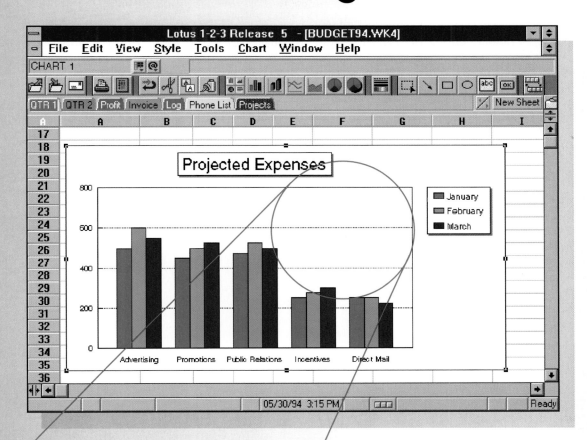

"Why would I do this?"

With 1-2-3, you can also add a grid to your chart. A grid appears in the plot area of the chart. Placing a grid on your chart makes it easier to interpret the chart's data. A grid is useful for emphasizing the y-axis scale of the data series.

Task 61: Adding Grid Lines

1 Click the chart border. This selects the entire chart. Click **Chart** in the menu bar. 1-2-3 opens the Chart menu and displays a list of Chart commands.

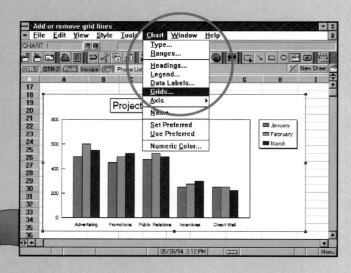

2 Click **Grids**. This selects the Grids command. 1-2-3 opens the Grids dialog box. Click the down arrow next to **Y-Axis**. Then, click Major Interval in the list. This selects the Major Interval grid lines option.

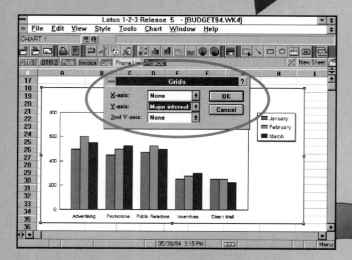

3 Click **OK**. 1-2-3 displays the lines across the chart.

WHY WORRY?

To remove the grid lines, immediately click the **Undo** SmartIcon. Or you can select **None** in the Grids dialog box to deselect any grid lines option.

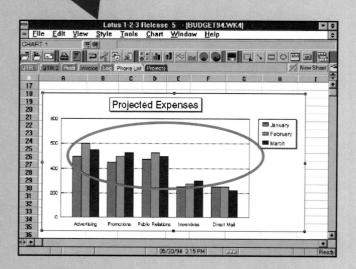

Changing Axis Scales

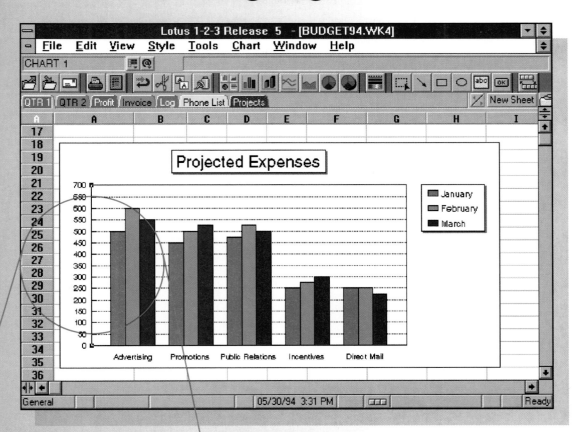

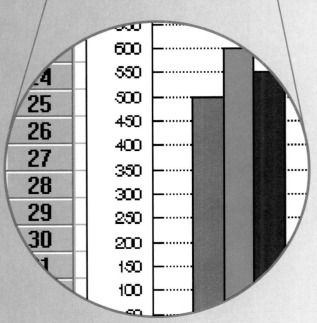

"Why would I do this?"

The vertical axis in a 1-2-3 chart is called the *y-axis*. 1-2-3 automatically scales the y-axis for your charts to best fit the minimum (lower value limit) and maximum (upper value limit) values being charted. But, sometimes you may need to customize the values along the vertical or horizontal axis. Perhaps you want to display more numbers in smaller increments on the value axis.

Task 62: Changing Axis Scales

1 Double-click the y-axis line (the vertical axis). 1-2-3 displays the Y-Axis dialog box. In the Scale Manually area, double-click in the **Upper Limit** text box and type **700**. This enters the high value on the y-axis—in this case, 700. An X appears in the Upper Limit check box, indicating that there is a manual scale change.

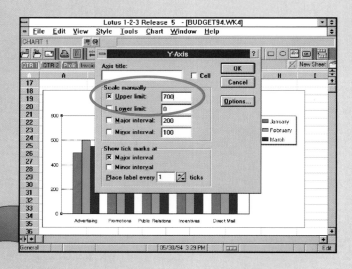

2 In the Scale Manually area, double-click in the **Major Interval** text box and type **50**. This enters the interval between values on the y-axis—in this case, 50. An X appears in the Major Interval check box, indicating that there is a manual scale change.

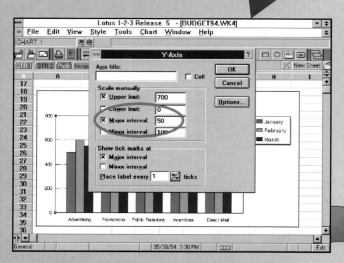

3 Click **OK**. This confirms your choices. As you can see, the highest value at the top of the y-axis is 700 and the interval between values is 50.

WHY WORRY?

If you don't get the scale numbers you want, just click the **Undo** SmartIcon. If you want to clear the settings and return to the original default values, repeat the previous steps.

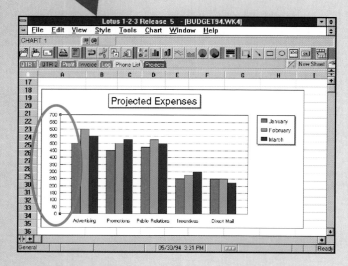

Formatting the Axes

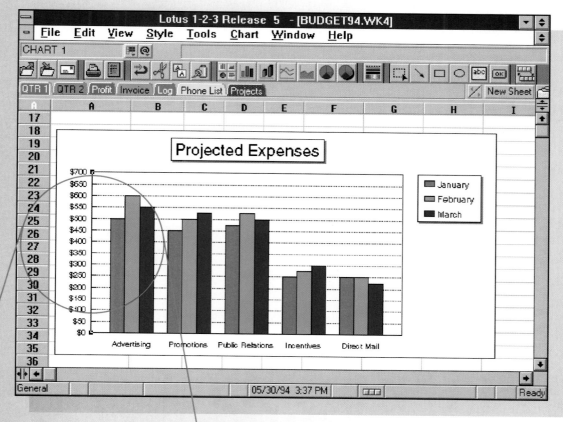

"Why would I do this?"

You can change the look of the scale indicators on the axes. For example, you can change the style, color, and weight of the axis line. You can change the format of the numbers that appear on the axis scale by adding dollar signs, decimal points, commas, and percent signs.

Task 63: Formatting the Axes

1 Click the vertical axis line, if necessary. This selects the value axis. Selection boxes (small black squares) appear at each end of the value axis.

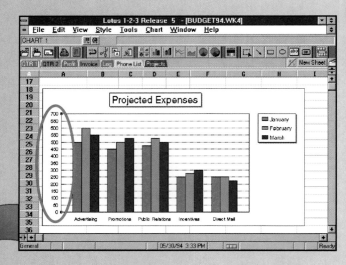

2 Click **Style** in the menu bar. This opens the Style menu. 1-2-3 displays a list of Style commands.

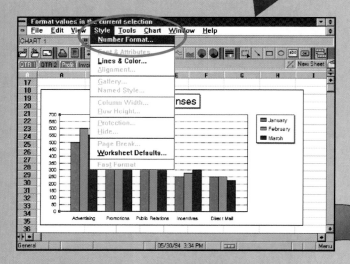

3 Click **Number Format**. This selects the Number Format command. 1-2-3 opens the Number Format dialog box.

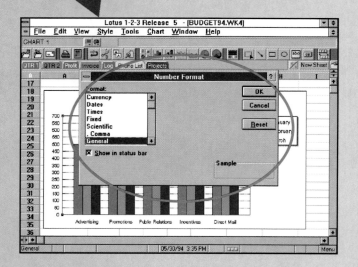

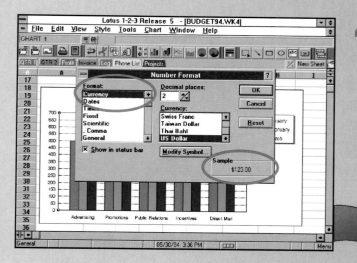

4 Click **Currency**. This selects the Currency format. This number format adds dollar signs and commas with two decimal places. The sample $123.00 appears in the lower right corner of the dialog box. Now change the decimal places to zero.

5 Click the down arrow next to the **Decimal Places** text box. Then, click the same down arrow again. Clicking this down arrow decreases the number of decimal places. The number of decimal places changes from two to zero.

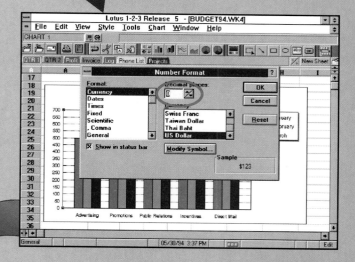

6 Click **OK**. This confirms your choice. 1-2-3 adds dollar signs to the values on the y-axis scale.

WHY WORRY?

If you don't get the results you want, click the **Undo** SmartIcon. Then repeat the previous steps and choose a different number format.

TASK 64

Changing the Patterns of Data Series

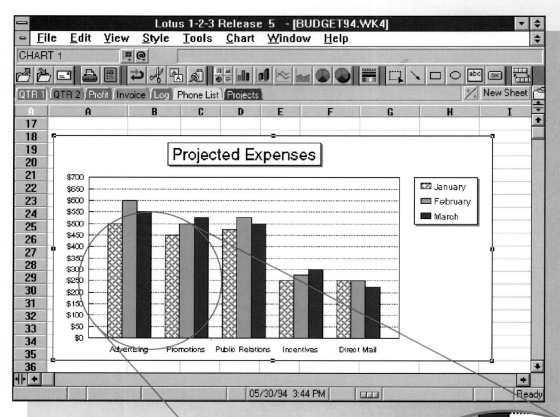

"Why would I do this?"

You may want to change the colors and patterns of the data series for special effects. When you change the patterns of data series, you may find some patterns and colors more attractive than others. For example, you may want to remove all patterns and use only color.

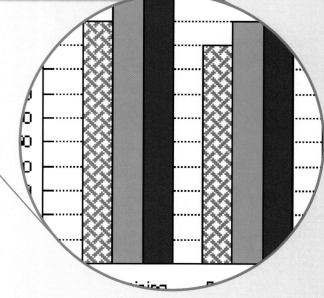

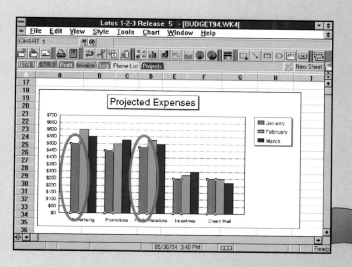

1 Click one of the first data series bars (the bars that represent January). This selects all the bars that represent the expenses for January. Small squares, or *selection boxes*, appear in each of the bars.

2 Click **Style** in the menu bar. This opens the Style menu. 1-2-3 displays a list of Style commands.

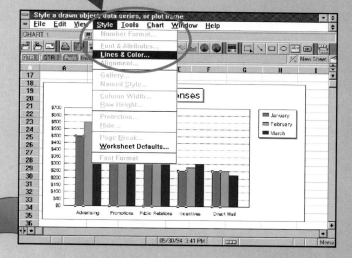

3 Click **Lines & Color**. This selects the Lines & Color command. 1-2-3 opens the Lines & Color dialog box.

4 From the Interior options, click the down arrow next to the **Pattern** text box. 1-2-3 displays a palette of patterns.

NOTE ▼

The Interior options control the inside of the element, such as its pattern and color. The Edge options affect the perimeter of the selected element, including the style, width, and color of the border line.

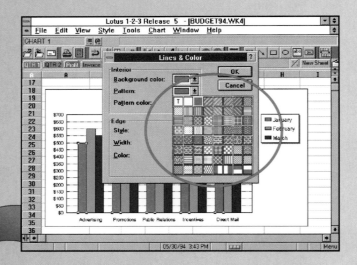

5 In the third row of the palette, click the fourth pattern from the left. This selects the lattice fence pattern. The sample appears on the right side of the dialog box.

6 Click **OK**. 1-2-3 displays the bars in the lattice fence pattern with the default color—in this case, red. Notice that the legend contains the new pattern for January.

WHY WORRY?

To remove the pattern from a data series, click the **Undo** SmartIcon. Then repeat the previous steps and choose a different pattern or a color.

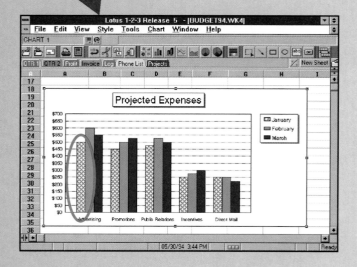

Creating a Map

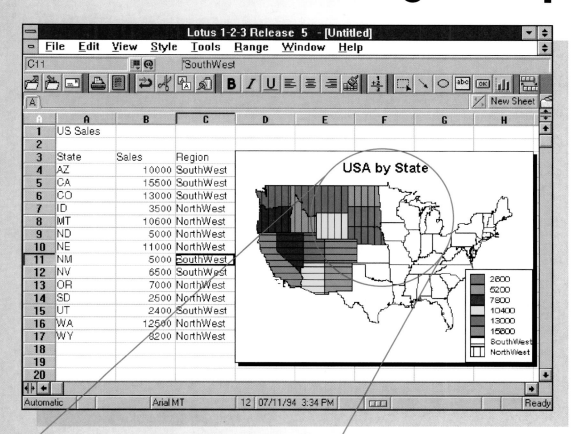

"Why would I do this?"

Maps are useful for charting numeric data that is defined by state, country, or province. Maps are not one of the chart types, but are a separate feature on the Tools menu. You can, for example, develop a sales map, automatically coloring the states based on up to six ranges of dollar amounts. Up to six patterns can be placed on a map to display a secondary data element, such as grouping by region name.

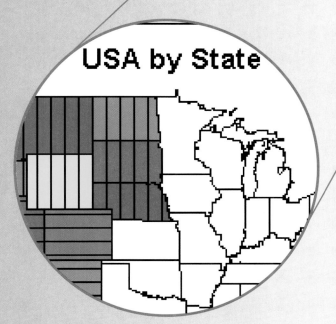

Task 65: Creating a Map

1 Type the information as displayed in this worksheet. To create a map, 1-2-3 requires a column of names or codes for states, countries, or provinces. The second column is the data that is linked on the map. The third column is optional; data in the third column is mapped as patterns. (The fourth column can be used for placing map pins, which you will not learn about here.)

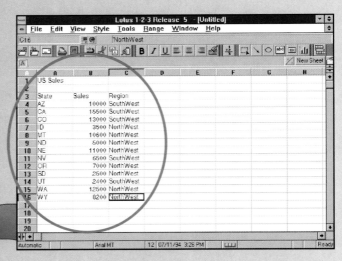

2 Select the range **A4** to **C16**. This selects the range A4..C16—the range you want to map. Click **Tools** in the menu bar, and then click **Map**. The Map menu options appear.

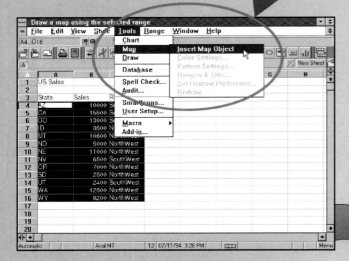

3 Click **Insert Map Object**. The title bar prompts you: Click where you want to display the map. The mouse pointer changes to a globe icon.

WHY WORRY?

If the Map Type dialog box appears first, select **USA by State**, and then click **OK.** Then the mouse pointer changes to a globe icon.

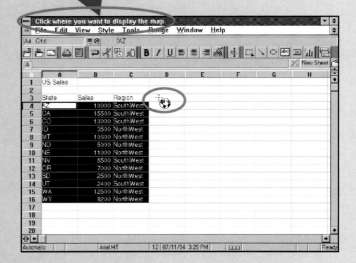

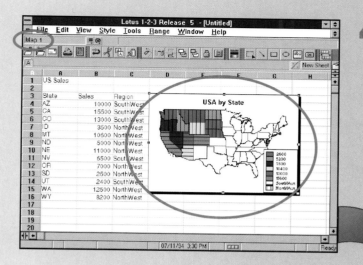

4 Click cell **D3**. You may have to wait several seconds while 1-2-3 composes the map. Then the map appears in the default size with its upper left corner in cell D3.

NOTE ▼

Map 1 appears in the selection indicator box. The legend shows the colors for upper limits of Sales and the pattern for Regions.

5 Move the map by clicking it and then dragging, or resize the map by dragging the selection handles.

NOTE ▼

As with charts, data that you change in the linked range is reflected as a change in the map.

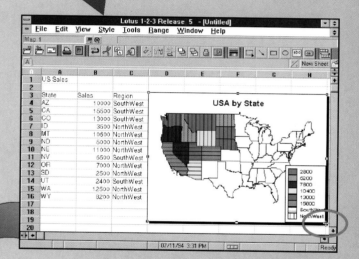

6 Insert a row at row 11. In cells **A11**, **B11**, and **C11**, type the data **NM**, **5000**, and **SouthWest**. The map changes automatically.

NOTE ▼

You can change the colors, patterns, title, and range of the map by choosing options in the Tools Map menu. You can change several other features of the map by using the Map Viewer, which is accessed by double-clicking anywhere on the map.

TASK 66

Printing a Map

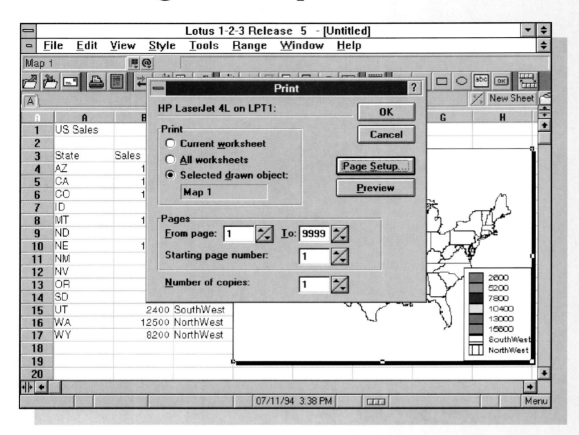

"Why would I do this?"

Printing a map is very much like printing a chart. You can print the map object by itself, or you can print it with the worksheet data to which it is linked. To print the map larger than it appears in the worksheet, you can change settings for size and orientation in Page Setup.

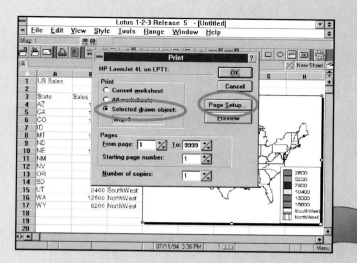

1 Select the map by clicking anywhere on the map. Selection handles will show. Click the **Print** SmartIcon to display the Print dialog box.

NOTE ▼

In the Print area, the Selected drawn object named **Map 1** is already selected for you.

2 Click the **Page Setup** button. In the Page Setup dialog box, select **Landscape** orientation. In the Size drop-down list, select Fill page but keep proportions.

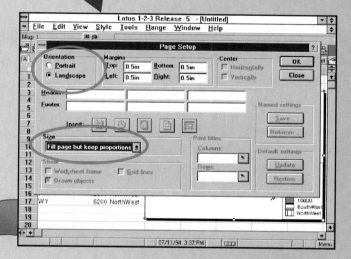

3 Click **OK** to return to the Print dialog box. Be sure your printer is ready, and then click **OK**. The full-page map prints in landscape orientation on your printer.

WHY WORRY?

Choose **Cancel** to stop printing the map while the message box is visible.

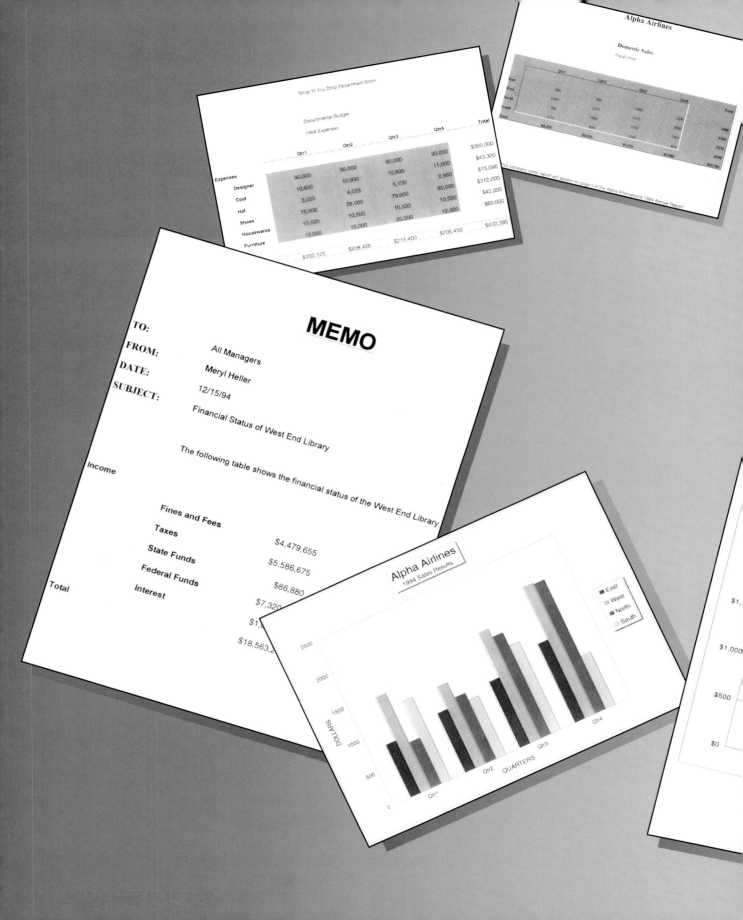

Alpha Airlines

Domestic Sales

Fiscal 1994

	Qtr1	Qtr2	Qtr3	Qtr4	
East		900	900		
West	7450		900		
North	700	1235	1000	1200	Total
South	1235	1000	1675	2000	3900
Total		490	1150		6360
	$4,201	$4,828	1345	1062	3250
			$5,670	810	4290
				$5,900	$19,700

This company sales report will appear on page 5 in the Alpha International 1994 Annual Report.

Shop 'til You Drop Department Store

Departmental Budget

1994 Expenses

	Qtr1	Qtr2	Qtr3	Qtr4	Total
				90,000	$360,000
Expenses		90,000	90,000	11,000	$43,300
Designer	90,000	10,900	10,800	2,950	$15,095
Coat	10,600	4,025	5,100	80,000	$312,000
Hat	3,020	78,000	79,000	10,500	$42,000
Shoes	75,000	10,500	10,500	12,000	$60,000
Housewares	10,500	15,000	20,000		$832,395
Furniture	13,000			$206,450	
	$202,120	$208,425	$215,400		

MEMO

TO: All Managers

FROM: Meryl Heller

DATE: 12/15/94

SUBJECT: Financial Status of West End Library

The following table shows the financial status of the West End Library.

Income

Fines and Fees	
Taxes	$4,479,655
State Funds	$5,586,675
Federal Funds	$86,880
Interest	$7,320
	$1,
Total	$18,563,2

Alpha Airlines

1994 Sales Results

Legend: East, West, North, South

Y-axis: DOLLARS (0, 500, 1000, 1500, 2000, 2500)

X-axis: QUARTERS (Qtr1, Qtr2, Qtr3, Qtr4)

$1,

$1,000

$500

$0

PART VIII

Sample Documents

▼ Create a Company Sales Report

▼ Create a Departmental Budget

▼ Create a Memo with a Table

▼ Create a Bar Chart

▼ Create an Expense Report and a Bar Chart

Times New Roman, 24 point bold

Times New Roman, 18 point bold

Chisel1 style template

Times New Roman, 14 point

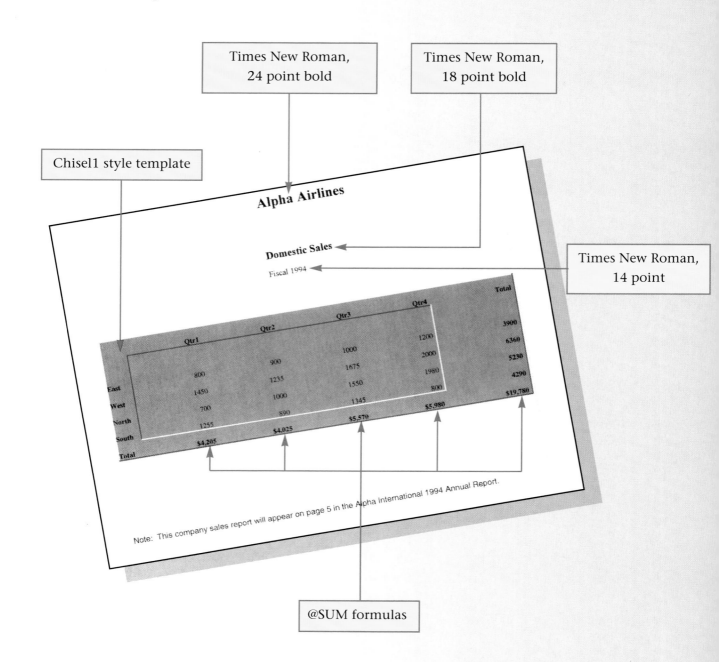

@SUM formulas

Create a Company Sales Report

1 Type the titles, column headings, row headings, and numbers. See these tasks for help on this step:

2 Enter a formula to add the first column of numbers. These tasks cover addition formulas:

3 Copy the formula across the total row. These tasks cover copying a formula:

4 Change the format of the column totals to US Dollar, 0 decimal places:

5 Change the format of the entire worksheet to the Chisel1 Format. See this task:

6 Save and print the sales report. See these tasks on saving and printing:

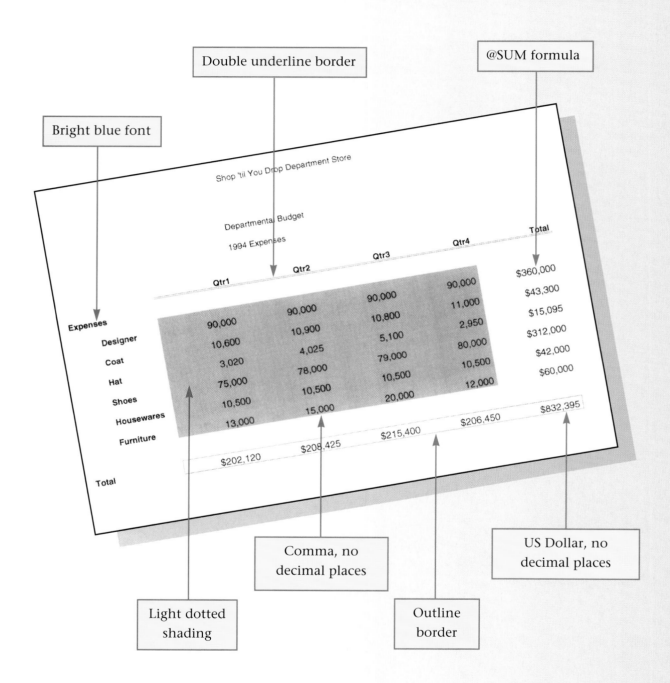

Double underline border

@SUM formula

Bright blue font

Shop 'til You Drop Department Store

Departmental Budget

1994 Expenses

	Qtr1	Qtr2	Qtr3	Qtr4	Total
Expenses				90,000	$360,000
Designer	90,000	90,000	90,000	11,000	$43,300
Coat	10,600	10,900	10,800	2,950	$15,095
Hat	3,020	4,025	5,100	80,000	$312,000
Shoes	75,000	78,000	79,000	10,500	$42,000
Housewares	10,500	10,500	10,500	12,000	$60,000
Furniture	13,000	15,000	20,000		
Total	$202,120	$208,425	$215,400	$206,450	$832,395

Comma, no decimal places

US Dollar, no decimal places

Light dotted shading

Outline border

Create a Departmental Budget

1 Type the information in the budget worksheet. See these tasks for help on this step:

2 Format the numbers for each quarter with commas and zero decimal places. Format the numbers in the total row and total column with dollar signs and zero decimal places. See this task:

3 Insert a double underline border beneath the column headings. Also, add an outline border to the numbers in the total row. See this task:

4 Change the font color of the column and row headings to bright blue (Color 136). See this task:

5 Add light dotted shading to the numbers in each column except for the total row and total column. See this task:

6 Save and print the budget. See these tasks on saving and printing:

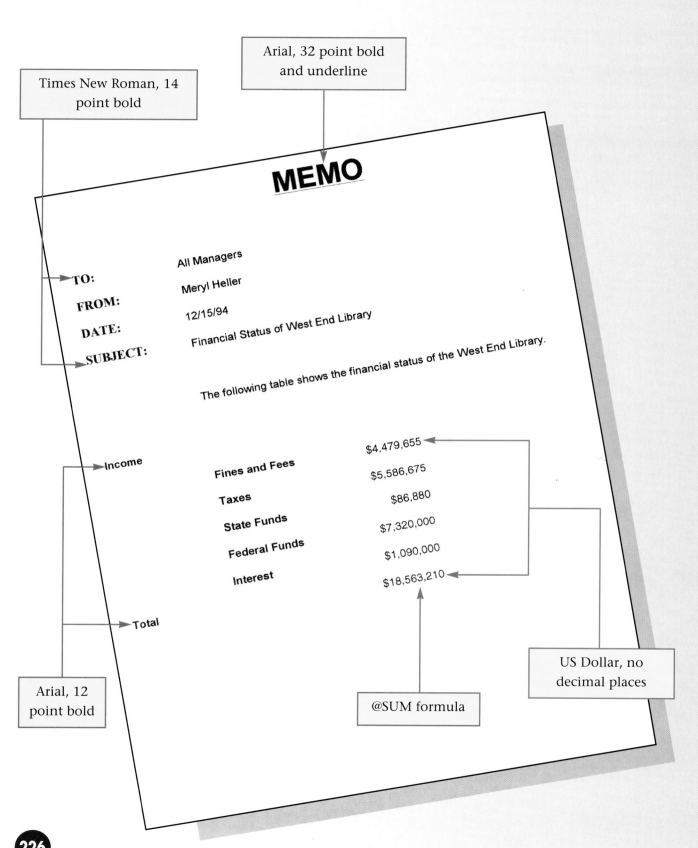

Arial, 32 point bold and underline

Times New Roman, 14 point bold

MEMO

TO: All Managers

FROM: Meryl Heller

DATE: 12/15/94

SUBJECT: Financial Status of West End Library

The following table shows the financial status of the West End Library.

Income	
Fines and Fees	$4,479,655
Taxes	$5,586,675
State Funds	$86,880
Federal Funds	$7,320,000
Interest	$1,090,000
Total	$18,563,210

Arial, 12 point bold

US Dollar, no decimal places

@SUM formula

Create a Memo with a Table

1 Type the memo, including the table. See these tasks for help on this step:

Entering Text and Numbers	*p. 30*
Changing the Font	*p. 149*
Adding Bold, Italic, and Underline	*p. 153*

2 Create an @SUM formula to add the numbers. See this task:

Totaling Cells with the @SUM Function	*p. 100*

3 Boldface and underline the title, MEMO. Change the font for the title to Arial, 32 point. Change the font for the memo headings to Times New Roman, 14 point. Then boldface the memo headings. Also, boldface the headings and subheadings in the table. These tasks cover font changes, bold, and underline:

Changing the Font	*p. 149*
Adding Bold, Italic, and Underline	*p. 153*

4 Format the totals with US Dollar and zero decimal places. See this task:

Displaying Dollar Signs, Commas, and Percent Signs	*p. 140*

5 Save and print the memo. See these tasks on saving and printing:

Saving and Closing a Worksheet	*p. 118*
Printing the Worksheet	*p. 184*

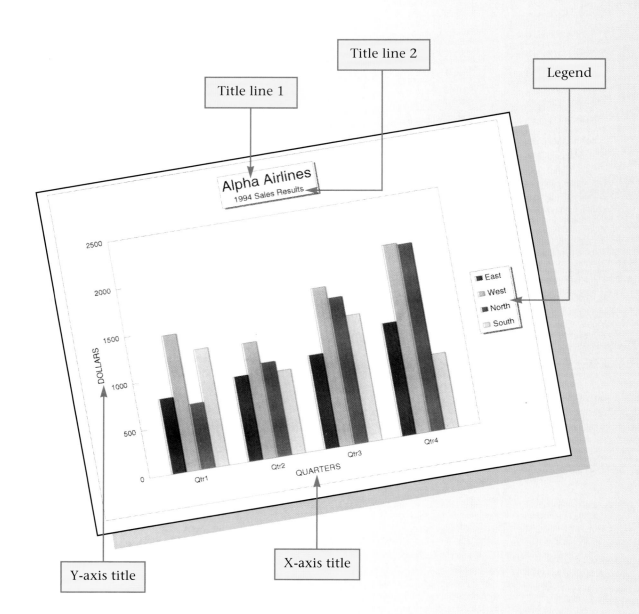

Title line 1

Title line 2

Legend

Y-axis title

X-axis title

Create a Bar Chart

1 Using the company sales report, create a bar chart on a separate sheet to show quarterly sales by territory. The data you want to chart includes the column headings, row headings, and sales figures. Do not include the totals. See these tasks for help on this step:

Selecting Cells	*p. 24*
Moving between Worksheets	*p. 20*
Creating a Chart	*p. 190*

2 Add the title Alpha Airlines and the subtitle 1994 Sales Results. See this task for help on this step:

Changing the Title	*p. 200*

3 Save and print the chart. See these tasks on saving and printing:

Saving and Closing a Worksheet	*p. 118*
Printing a Chart	*p. 192*

Part VIII: Sample Documents

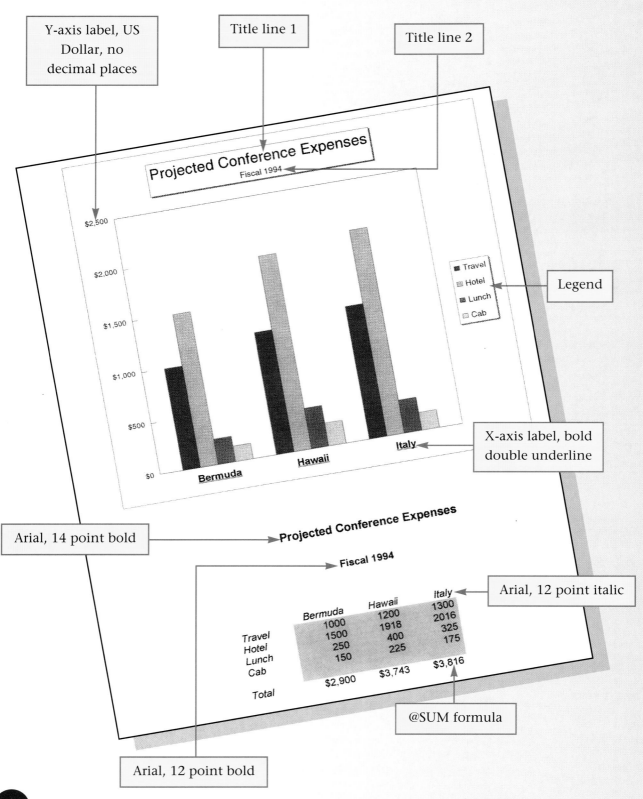

230

Create an Expense Report and a Bar Chart

1 Type the expense report in the worksheet. See these tasks for help on this step:

Entering Text and Numbers   *p. 30*

Adding Bold, Italic, and Underline   *p. 153*

2 Enter a formula to add the expenses in each column. See these tasks:

Adding Data with a Formula   *p. 86*

Totaling Cells with the @SUM Function   *p. 100*

3 Copy the formula across the total row. These tasks cover copying a formula:

Filling a Range   *p. 51*

Copying a Formula   *p. 106*

4 Select the data you want to chart: the column headings, row headings, and expenses. Do not include the totals. Then create a bar chart on the worksheet. See these tasks for help on this step:

Selecting Cells   *p. 24*

Creating a Chart   *p. 190*

5 Save and print the expense report and the bar chart. See these tasks on saving and printing:

Saving and Closing a Worksheet   *p. 118*

Printing the Worksheet   *p. 184*

PART IX

Reference

▼ Quick Reference

▼ SmartIcons Guide

Quick Reference

If you cannot remember how to access a particular feature, use this list to find the appropriate command. For more detailed information, see the tasks in Parts I through VII of this book.

Feature	Command	Shortcut Key
Alignment	Style Alignment	(none)
Bold	Style Font & Attributes	**Ctrl+B**
Border	Style Lines & Color	(none)
Center Data	Style Alignment	**Ctrl+E**
Clear Cell	Edit Clear	**Del**
Close File	File Close	**Ctrl+F4**
Column Delete	Edit Delete Column	**Ctrl+−** (numeric keypad)
Column Hide	Style Hide	(none)
Column Insert	Edit Insert Column	**Ctrl++** (numeric keypad)
Column Width	Style Column Width	(none)
Copy	Edit Copy	**Ctrl+C**
Edit Cell	(none)	**F2**
Exit	File Exit	**Alt+F4**
Font	Style Font & Attributes	Status bar (4th panel)
Format Numbers	Style Number Format	Status bar (1st panel)
Go To	Edit Go To	**F5**
Help	Help	**F1**
Italic	Style Font & Attributes	**Ctrl+I**

Feature	Command	Shortcut Key
Left-Align Data	Style Alignment	**Ctrl+L**
Move	Edit Cut, then Edit Paste	**Ctrl+X**, then **Ctrl+V**
New File	File New	(none)
Open File	File Open	**Ctrl+O**
Page Break	Style Page Break	(none)
Preview	File Print Preview	(none)
Print	File Print	**Ctrl+P**
Range Fill	Range Fill by Example	(none)
Range Name	Range Name Create	(none)
Replace	Edit Replace	(none)
Right-Align Data	Style Alignment	**Ctrl+R**
Row Delete	Edit Delete Row	**Ctrl+−** (numeric keypad)
Row Height	Style Row Height	(none)
Row Hide	Style Hide	(none)
Row Insert	Edit Insert Row	**Ctrl++** (numeric keypad)
Save	File Save	**Ctrl+S**
Save As	File Save As	(none)
Shade	Style Lines & Color	(none)
Sort Data	Range Sort	(none)
Underline	Style Font & Attributes	**Ctrl+U**
Undo	Edit Undo	**Ctrl+Z**

SmartIcons Guide

The SmartIcons appear near the top of the 1-2-3 screen. They let you accomplish many 1-2-3 tasks more quickly. To use a SmartIcon, simply click the icon. To view a description of a SmartIcon, position the mouse pointer over the SmartIcon. The description appears in a "bubble" next to the SmartIcon. The following table lists the SmartIcons in the default palette.

SmartIcon	Name	Purpose
	File Open	Opens a worksheet
	File Save	Saves a worksheet
	Send Mail	Sends data by electronic mail
	Print	Prints a worksheet
	Print Preview	Previews a print job
	Undo	Undoes the preceding action
	Cut	Cuts a range to the Clipboard
	Copy	Copies a range to the Clipboard
	Paste	Pastes a range
	Bold	Makes cell contents bold
	Italic	Makes cell contents italic
	Underline	Makes cell contents underlined
	Left Align	Aligns cell entries to the left
	Center	Centers entries in a cell
	Right Align	Aligns cell entries to the right
	Fast Format	Copies a range's style
	Sum	Inserts an @SUM function

SmartIcon	Name	Purpose
	Select Objects	Selects objects
	Arrow	Draws an arrow
	Ellipse	Draws an ellipse or circle
	Text Block	Draws a text block
	Macro Button	Draws a macro button
	Create Chart	Creates a vertical bar chart
	Select SmartIcons	Displays next set of SmartIcons

Index

Symbols

A

B

C

Index